Motivating:

Helping Staff Achieve Peak Performance

ACA
FOUNDED 1870

About the Authors

Lydia Banks is a professional writer and marketing consultant who has collaborated with a number of major U.S. corporations.

Adapted for the American Correctional Association by **Ida M. Halasz**, Ph.D., who served as the Deputy Administrator of the National Institute of Corrections Academy, U.S. Department of Justice. Currently, as Vice President of Powell International Inc., she provides training and consulting services to public and private sector organizations.

ISBN 1-56991-100-2

a publication of the
AMERICAN CORRECTIONAL ASSOCIATION
Professional Development Department
4380 Forbes Boulevard
Lanham, Maryland 20706-4322
(301) 918-1800
Fax: (301) 918-1900
http://www.corrections.com/ACA

Foreword

The management of jails, prisons, and juvenile facilities has grown into a very complex task in recent years. At one time, corrections was largely a matter of preventing escapes, providing discipline as wardens and security staff saw fit, and providing a few of the basic necessities of life in an environment largely isolated from society. The range of skills needed was limited.

Today, the management of correctional facilities requires an understanding of a variety of technologies, staff relations, medical and psychiatric care, the legal system, information systems, employee unions, and media relations. Corrections must handle an exploding inmate population and at the same time deal with continual assault by courts and the media. The operation of jail and prison facilities must take careful account of detailed court orders, national standards for health and safety, and the oversight of numerous federal, state, and local agencies, often in an environment of stagnant or even declining financial resources.

In this current environment, success or failure rests almost entirely on the shoulders of an overworked and often underpaid staff. Motivating staff is therefore a key ingredient in the operation of a safe and humane institution. Of all segments of the criminal justice system, the corrections worker's job is the poorest understood by the public and often the least respected. Sheriffs and state corrections officials can strive to better inform the public about the vital contribution their deputies and correctional officers make to public safety. But correctional workers will always earn less respect from the media and the public than they deserve for the difficult and dangerous job they do. Managers must develop a set of tools for motivating staff that offers the workers a sense of involvement and personal investment in the goals of the organization. Correctional workers must feel a vital part of a team, or better yet, a family.

Achieving this kind of motivation requires skills and an understanding of what works and what doesn't. This workbook is a valuable resource for training correctional supervisors and managers in motivating their staff. It is both comprehensive and accessible and is an important contribution to the educational and training literature provided by the American Correctional Association.

Charles C. Foti Jr.
Orleans Parish Criminal Sheriff

Introduction

Inspiring staff motivation requires much more than the old-fashioned carrot-and-stick approach. Today's correctional supervisor or manager needs to understand the reasons why staff work and offer the rewards staff hope to receive.

This workbook will introduce you to the many factors that affect staff motivation. As you read, you'll discover:

What staff expect from work (it's more than just money)

How a correctional supervisor's vision and values inspire staff

Effective ways to reward your staff

The importance of creating a supportive workplace

The role open communication plays in maintaining motivation

How to deal with unmotivated staff

Once you're done, you'll be ready to inspire your staff in dozens of ways and create a work environment that will support their desire to achieve.

Table of Contents

Chapter Four

Rewarding Your Staff

Chapter Five

Maintaining A Positive Work Environment

Chapter Six

Maintaining Open Communication

Chapter Seven

Dealing With Unmotivated Staff

Chapter One

WHAT IS MOTIVATION?

Chapter Objectives

After completing this chapter, you should be able to:

- Explain the nature of staff motivation.
- Explain the importance of creating a workplace that inspires and supports staff motivation.
- Identify aspects of today's workplace that can affect staff motivation.

Most of us have seen people who perform their jobs by doing as little as possible. They come to work late and leave early. They miss deadlines, and when they complete a task, they do only the minimum required. They can often be found spending some extra time in the break room complaining about their jobs.

Supervisors and managers can create an environment that inspires and supports staff motivation.

We also know people who give 110 percent to their jobs. They're punctual and hardworking, and they approach new projects with a smile instead of a complaint. What makes these two types of workers so different? The answer is *motivation*.

Motivated staff have a will to succeed, a drive to do their best no matter what the project. Unmotivated staff are less concerned about their performance and willing to get by with a minimum amount of effort.

As a supervisor or manager, you want to develop and encourage good staff performance, and good performance comes from strong staff motivation. But supervisors and managers can't *motivate* staff. Motivation is an internal state—like emotions and attitudes—that only the individual can control. Correctional supervisors and managers *can*, however, create a workplace environment that will inspire and support strong motivation on the part of their staff. That is what we will explore in this workbook. Specifically, we will consider how correctional supervisors and managers can:

- Create a workplace that helps staff satisfy psychological needs as well as the need for income.
- Set clear goals for staff performance.
- Encourage good performance through rewards and reinforcement.
- Maintain open communication with all staff.

We will explore these techniques in the following chapters. But before we begin, let's take a look at some of the unique features of today's correctional workplace and how those features affect motivation.

Take a Moment . . .

Think of a situation in which you felt motivated to do your very best. Can you identify any aspect of that situation that inspired and supported your motivation? Describe it below:

Motivation in the Corrections Workplace

Motivation in today's workplace is affected by a number of factors, including:

- A decreasing emphasis on money
- An increasing amount of work
- An increasing need to work together in teams

Placing Less Emphasis on Money

For many years, traditional wisdom held that staff worked primarily for money and could be "motivated" through a combination of financial rewards and fear. Within this perspective, supervisors or managers might offer financial rewards as their only performance incentive. They also might try to generate fear by threatening to fire or demote staff if they did not perform at a certain level.

What does a good job provide?

- **Job satisfaction**
- **Time for family life**
- **Money**

Today, we realize that our reasons for performing well on the job are far more complex. Though we often define a good job as a well-paying job, many of us would also consider other issues, such as job satisfaction and time for a family life.

Patrick is a case in point. When he began his job as a parole officer, he was excited about opportunities to move up in the organization. He worked hard and was promoted several times.

As Patrick's income grew, so did his family's possessions. First, they bought a new car, then a bigger house, then more furniture.

Patrick worked hard with many hours of

overtime to get the job done. But after a few years, he began to become dissatisfied. He had acquired a good lifestyle but barely saw his family all week and was tired of the long hours. He wished for different challenges and time to spend with his children before they grew up and left home.

Situations like Patrick's are more common than you might think. Many of today's workers are not primarily motivated by a desire for money. They crave a deeper satisfaction from their jobs and won't respond to old-style supervision or management techniques.

Take a Moment . . .

Why do you work? Does the thought of more money inspire you to do your best, or do other rewards inspire you more? List some of the factors that help you increase your motivation.

Today's correctional workers face an increased workload.

Dealing with Greater Amounts of Work

One of the primary challenges facing today's correctional worker is an increased workload. Workforces have been downsized. Technology has pushed workers to a faster pace. The result is that staff must learn a variety of new tasks and use their minds and bodies at a faster rate than ever before. Though these changes may bring many benefits, the stress involved in any change can affect staff motivation.

Take a Moment . . .

Have increased workloads or changes in tasks affected your staff in the past year or two? List some of the effects you've noticed below:

____

____

____

____

____

____

____

For many correctional workers, home life can be just as busy as the workplace. Completing housework and laundry, juggling day care, preparing meals, and supervising homework can create what amounts to a second workday at home. Because many baby boomers married and started families late in life, they may be faced with added challenges. They may be raising small children at the same time that they are given increased supervisory or managerial responsibilities at work.

For many correctional workers, home life can be just as busy as the workplace.

Here is a log of a typical evening compiled by a married staff member with young children. It was created to illustrate how much activity a parent can encounter after a long day at work.

5:25 P.M.	Pick up Annie at day care.
5:45	Pick up Jonathan at after-school care.
6:00	Arrive home. Set table as children wash hands.
6:12	Answer phone; salesperson calling.
6:13	Help Annie, who has slipped on bathroom floor.
6:14	Look at Jonathan's schoolwork while getting out food and pouring drinks.
6:18	Greet spouse, who complains about fast-food dinner.
6:20	Settle fight after Annie throws french fries at Jonathan.
6:25	Answer phone. Mother asks when family is coming to visit.

To continue would take up several pages of this workbook! It's easy to see how a staff member so busy at home could feel tired and unmotivated at work. Is your home life as busy as the example above? Keep a log of a typical evening with the blank log provided below, then log a typical morning.

Typical P.M. Time Log

noon-12:30 ______________________________

12:30-1:00 ______________________________

1:00-1:30 ______________________________

1:30-2:00 ______________________________

2:00-2:30 ______________________________

2:30-3:00 ______________________________

3:00-3:30 ______________________________

3:30-4:00 ______________________________

4:00-4:30 ______________________________

4:30-5:00 ______________________________

5:00-5:30 ______________________________

5:30-6:00 ______________________________

6:00-6:30 ______________________________

6:30-7:00 ______________________________

7:00-7:30 ______________________________

7:30-8:00 ______________________________

8:00-8:30 ______________________________

8:30-9:00 ______________________________

9:00-9:30 ______________________________

9:30-10:00 ______________________________

10:00-10:30 ______________________________

10:30-11:00 ______________________________

11:00-11:30 ______________________________

11:30-midnight ______________________________

Typical A.M. Time Log

midnight-12:30 ______________________________

12:30-1:00 ______________________________

1:00-1:30 ______________________________

1:30-2:00 ______________________________

2:00-2:30 ______________________________

2:30-3:00 ______________________________

3:00-3:30 ______________________________

3:30-4:00 ______________________________

4:00-4:30 ______________________________

4:30-5:00 ______________________________

5:00-5:30 ______________________________

5:30-6:00 ______________________________

6:00-6:30 ______________________________

6:30-7:00 ______________________________

7:00-7:30 ______________________________

7:30-8:00 ______________________________

8:00-8:30 ______________________________

8:30-9:00 ______________________________

9:00-9:30 ______________________________

9:30-10:00 ______________________________

10:00-10:30 ______________________________

11:00-11:30 ______________________________

11:30-noon ______________________________

Personal Time Log

____

____

____

____

____

____

____

____

____

____

____

Take a Moment . . .

How does your home life affect your work life?

Do you think other staff in your department have similar concerns?

Working in Teams

The *amount of work* isn't the only aspect of the workplace that has recently changed—*the way people work together* has changed as well. Today's workers are increasingly asked to work in teams, and this can have both positive and negative effects on motivation. If staff members are able to build a strong team relationship, their shared sense of commitment can inspire motivation on the part of individual members. But poor dynamics could discourage motivation. For example, the team may experience a number of conflicts, or individual members may believe their efforts are ignored or undervalued.

Take a Moment . . .

Does your organization or department have a number of work teams? If so, how do you think team dynamics are affecting the motivation of individual team members?

Encouraging the Desire to Succeed

This workbook takes the perspective that people are inherently well-meaning and *want* to do a good job. Even those people who currently perform their duties in a lackluster manner have some desire for success; it simply isn't manifesting itself in their job situation.

Motivated staff have a drive to succeed, no matter what the job.

By providing the right kind of support, correctional supervisors and managers can develop and encourage staff to succeed. But staff members must bring something to the equation as well—open minds and the willingness to work with supervisors and managers to make changes that will improve the workplace and their own performance. Working together, supervisors, managers, and staff can create an environment in which everyone feels motivated to give every challenge her or his best effort.

Summary

Motivated staff have a drive to succeed, no matter what the job. Correctional supervisors and managers cannot "motivate" staff, but they *can* create a work environment that inspires and supports strong staff motivation.

As correctional supervisors and managers strive to create a good work environment, they should be aware of several features of today's workplace that can affect staff motivation:

- A decreasing emphasis on money
- An increasing amount of work
- An increasing need to work together in teams

By taking these and other factors into account, supervisors and managers can create an environment that encourages staffs' desire to succeed. But staff must also contribute to this effort by keeping an open mind and working with their supervisors to improve the work environment and their performance.

Working in teams can have both positive and negative effects on motivation.

Chapter One Review

Answers to these questions appear on page 109.

1. True/False. Correctional managers and supervisors can motivate staff.
2. Today's correctional workers place an ____________ on work and working together in teams.
3. True/False. Fear is an effective way to encourage motivation.
4. For many correctional workers, _______and the__________are equally hectic.
5. When do team situations discourage staff motivation?

____

____

____

____

____

____

____

____

Chapter Two

WHY DO WE WORK?

Chapter Objectives

After completing this chapter, you should be able to:

- Explain the nature of staff motivation.
- Describe the importance of creating a workplace that inspires and supports staff motivation.
- Identify aspects of today's workplace that can affect staff motivation.

Why do we work?
- **Survival**
- **Fill needs**

Why do we work? What makes us struggle out of bed every morning, stumble through breakfast, and fight rush hour traffic? It would be so much easier to spend the day in front of the TV with a bowl of popcorn.

Survival is part of the answer. We work to eat, buy clothes, pay our rent or mortgage. But survival is only one of the reasons we work. We work in order to meet many different needs. The more needs our jobs can help us meet, the more our motivation to perform well is encouraged. Understanding why people work—and what needs they hope to fill—can help supervisors and managers determine what they can do to appeal to those needs and inspire staff motivation.

Take a Moment . . .

Why do you think you work? Is survival the only reason, or do you work for something more:

List some of the reasons you work below:

What Are Our Needs?

Humans are complex creatures with a variety of needs. Some of our needs—like the need for air, water, food, and shelter—are basic and necessary for physical survival. Others, like the need for love and companionship, are psychological and emotional. Abraham Maslow developed a useful model for categorizing human needs. As you can see in the figure below, Maslow organized human needs into a hierarchy with the needs most basic to survival on the bottom. Maslow suggested that once we fill our basic needs, we can progress up the hierarchy to focus on emotional satisfaction and self-fulfillment.

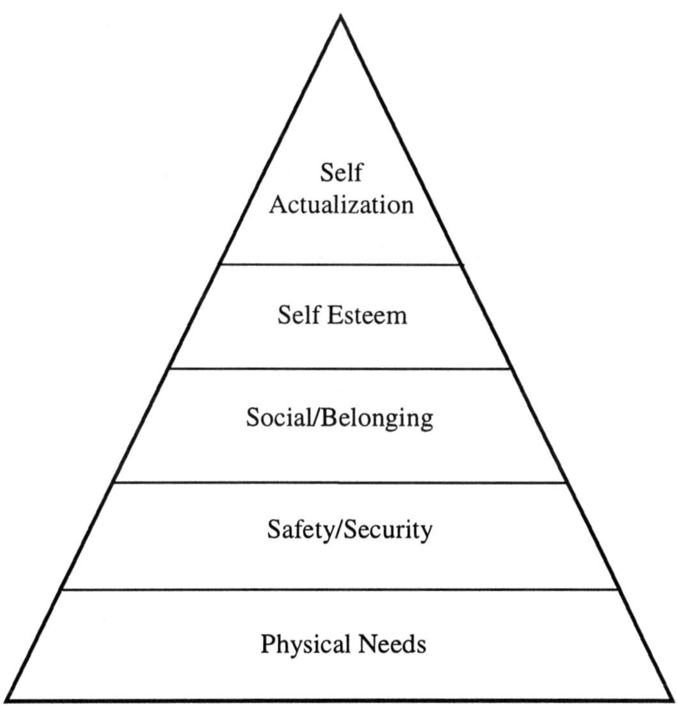

We have many different ways of filling the categories of needs described by Maslow. Here are some ways they are met in modern society.

NEED	DESCRIPTION	HOW NEED IS MET IN MODERN SOCIETY
Physical	Elements needed for physical survival	Clean air and water, food, sleep, sex
Safety/Security	Protection from harm	Shelter, warning systems, security systems, laws and law enforcement
Social/Belonging	Companionship and affection	Social groups, social events, shared tasks, mating, family
Self-esteem	Concern with how one feels about him- or herself	Position in family, community, or work; feeling of self-worth
Self-Actualization	Feeling of achieving one's best	Education, therapy, meditation, decision-making power, control over one's life, ability to produce desired outcomes

Take a Moment . . .

Go over the categories of human needs and how they can be filled. Can you think of ways in which the workplace can help people meet these needs? List them below:

Physical/Physiological ____________________

____

____

____

Safety/Security ____________________________

____

____

____

Social/Belonging ___________________________

____

____

____

Self-Esteem ________________________________

____

____

____

Self-Actualization _________________________

____

____

This list of the ways our needs can be met is by no means exhaustive, but you may have already begun to see its relationship to the correc-

Needs filled → Feel motivated

tions workplace. When staffs' needs for food, shelter, security, and status are met, they will feel more motivated than when those needs are not met. Supervisors and managers can meet staff needs in a number of ways, through income and the work environment itself.

Meeting Needs Through Income

Staff members with steady incomes can meet physical needs for food and shelter and security needs for clean, safe neighborhoods. A good-sized income can help staff acquire items that help them meet status needs, such as a new car or a bigger house. It can also give staff the leisure time to pursue self-actualization through hobbies or other forms of self-expression.

As we will discuss later in this chapter, supervisors and managers can use income in many ways to inspire motivation. But income isn't the only way the workplace can fill staff needs. The work environment itself can satisfy many staff needs.

Meeting Needs Through Work Environment

The following list includes just a few ways in which staff needs may be satisfied at work:

Physical needs—A workplace meets staffs' physical needs by providing comfortable work spaces with clean air, good lighting, and appropriate room temperatures. Even the most positive attitude can be damaged by a dark, uncomfortable work environment.

Security needs—Staff members who are

worried about their physical safety can't concentrate on work and can suffer undue stress. Correctional supervisors and managers can meet staff security needs by taking all possible precautions against violence, harassment, and physical danger. Supervisors and managers can also meet staff security needs by doing the following:

- protecting jobs through fair personnel and salary decisions
- providing extra incentives, such as lists of certified child-care providers

Social needs—Correctional supervisors and managers don't pay workers to socialize. However, many social needs can be met at work through the opportunity to work on teams and participate in group activities. Strong team relationships encourage strong staff motivation.

Professional achievement = Increased self-esteem

Self-Esteem—Work offers the possibility of promotion and the opportunity to progress through various ranks and salary levels. Staff members are much more motivated to work when they don't perceive themselves as holding "dead end" jobs.

Self-Actualization—Work provides staff with interesting assignments that allow them to grow professionally and personally. As staff members become self-actualized, they accept more responsibility for their performance and receive more control over their activities.

One final way that the workplace can help staff meet their needs is by providing them the flexibility to take care of issues in other areas of their lives. As Maslow's list of needs suggests, our work and personal lives are not as neatly separated as we might like.

In the correctional workplace, security and safety are extremely important as a basis for motivation on the job. A staff member who constantly feels threatened will not be as motivated as a staff member who believes there are adequate security measures when working with inmates.

Placing a staff member on a different shift can enable a correctional worker to resolve personal problems and inspire motivation.

Take a Moment . . . 

Can you think of some way in which your facility currently fills staff needs? List them below. Can you think of any additional ways your facility might fill staff needs in the future? List those too.

Physical
(e.g., new equipment)

____

____

Safety/Security
(e.g., training in staff safety)

____

____

Social/Belonging
(e.g., team projects)

____

____

Self-Esteem
(e.g., mentoring program)

____

____

Self-Actualization
(e.g., individual projects)

____

Other Work-Based Needs

Psychologist David McClelland provides another way of categorizing the needs people hope to satisfy through their work. He identified three types of work-based needs:

1. The need for love
2. The need for achievement
3. The need for power

According to McClelland, not everyone has the same level of need for each particular area. A *dominant* person might have a strong need for power and a secondary need for achievement, but little need for love. The *sociable* worker's greatest need may be for association with others, rather than power. A worker with *low self-esteem* might focus on achievement but be too shy to seek power or love.

Once again, there are numerous ways in which correctional supervisors and managers can help staff meet these needs, including:

- Creating work teams to increase the opportunity for love or caring for others as human beings (in a social sense)
- Developing challenging work assignments that will increase the opportunity for achievement
- Giving staff more control over their own work situations as a means of empowerment

Take a Moment . . .

How would you rank your work-based needs? Use a scale of 1, 2, and 3.

_________ Love/caring

_________ Achievement

_________ Power

Why do you believe this?

____

____

____

____

As Maslow's and McClelland's theories suggest, we work for a complex variety of reasons beyond financial compensation. Correctional supervisors and managers can encourage staff motivation by recognizing staff's needs and providing ways to meet them.

How Much Power Does Money Have?

As we have seen, people work to fill a variety of needs, both material and psychological. Money can certainly help us meet a number of these needs, but how does it affect our motivation? Perhaps not as dramatically as we might think. In his research, theorist Frederick Herzberg found that increased money did not necessarily lead to increased worker motivation. It did, however, reduce the level of staff complaints.

Some of your staff may place a high value

on money, while others may not, for a variety of reasons, including:

- **They may not need much money**. A single worker whose home is paid off and who makes a car last 120,000 miles will have far lower living expenses than someone with two new cars, a mortgage, and children in day care. A staff member without pressing financial needs might value time off or public recognition more than money.
- **They value other factors more than money**. Some people place a greater emphasis on other factors, such as integrity, values, personal expression, or intellectual challenge. A vegetarian wouldn't work in a meat-processing plant, no matter what the salary, and a dancer would be dissatisfied with a desk job, even if it meant a substantial raise.

While some staff members may place a high value on money, many others do not.

Even those workers who do place a substantial value on money are beginning to question their priorities. As author Timothy Miller points out in his book *How to Want What You Have*, these people are beginning to realize that constantly striving for more money and possessions will not bring satisfaction for the following reasons:

- Gaining more does not eliminate sorrow, humiliation, pain, or death.
- Desiring more often does harm.
- Striving for more is not always enjoyable.
- Desiring more ignores spiritual longing.

As more people question their desire for money, correctional supervisors and managers will need to use other aspects of the work environment to inspire motivation. Rather than a pay increase, correctional workers might wish for more challenging, less repetitive jobs and more opportunities to enjoy leisure time or care for their families.

Take a Moment . . .

If you could name one thing that would most inspire your motivation to perform well in the workplace, what would it be? Money? Something else?

____

____

____

Your Role as a Leader

Where money truly rates as a staff motivator varies with who's telling the story. A study conducted by *Industry Week* magazine found that it fell in the second slot. This survey of approximately 2,500 workers asked for the primary long-term motivator. The answers:

Having a leader with vision and values	32.6%
Getting pay raises and bonuses	27.5%
Gaining greater responsibility	20.7%
Gaining respect of peers and subordinates	16.6%
Achieving recognition from supervisor(s)	12.5%
Other	8.7%

The number one support for staff motivation seems to be the influence of the leader. Clearly, workers respect a leader with vision. As a correctional supervisor or manager, your leadership plays a vital role in encouraging your staff. In the next chapter, we'll consider how you can provide strong leadership and supervision by setting goals for your staff. The goals you set will clarify staff roles and inspire their motivation.

Summary

People work for a variety of reasons. Our incomes provide us with the food and shelter we need to survive. However, our jobs also help us fill a number of psychological and emotional needs.

Abraham Maslow developed a model that places human needs in a hierarchy, as in this figure:

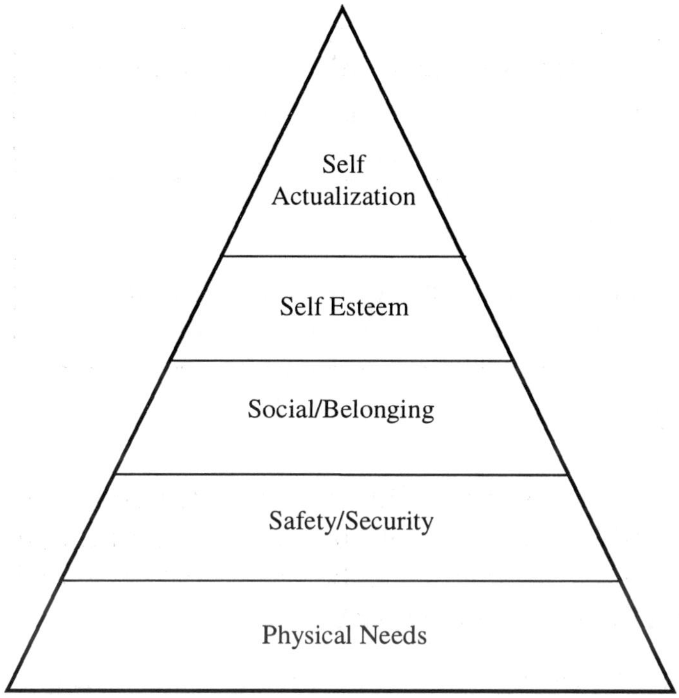

People work for a variety of reasons.

According to Maslow, as we fill our basic needs, we are able to progress up the hierarchy until we deal with concerns about self-fulfillment needs. Our jobs can help us meet many of these needs, both through the income they provide and the opportunities for social contact and challenging work.

Another model developed by David McClelland considers just those needs that are met by the workplace. These include:

1. The need for love or caring for others as human beings
2. The need for achievement

3. The need for power

Not everyone has the same level of need for each particular area.

Money can help us meet many of our needs, but money alone does not always encourage increased motivation. Many correctional workers may not need much money or may value other things more. As Timothy Miller suggests, some workers are discovering that constantly striving for more money and possessions is unfulfilling.

Money can contribute to a supportive work environment. But research suggests its influence on staff motivation is secondary compared to the vision and values of a group leader. As a correctional supervisor or manager, your leadership plays a vital role in encouraging your staff and inspiring their motivation.

Chapter Two Review

Answers to these questions appear on pages 109–110.

1. What are the five categories of human needs identified by Abraham Maslow?

   ____

   ____

   ____

   ____

   ____

2. True/False. Staff members who are worried about their physical safety can't concentrate on work and can suffer undue stress.

3. Working in ____________ can provide us with the opportunity to meet our social needs.

4. According to David McClelland, what three types of needs do people hope to satisfy specifically through work?

   ____

   ____

   ____

5. As more people question their desire for _______________, correctional supervisors and managers will need to use other aspects of the work environment to inspire motivation.

Chapter Three

ESTABLISHING YOUR VISION

Chapter Objectives

After completing this chapter, you should be able to:

- Develop a vision to inspire your department or team.
- Set goals to help your department or team live out its vision.
- Measure staff progress in meeting goals.
- Identify the factors that inspire ongoing staff motivation for Continuous Improvement.

Convey to your staff a clear vision of what you hope your organization, division, department, or team will achieve.

The number one factor that inspires staff motivation is a supervisor or manager with vision. This makes your challenge as a correctional supervisor or manager clear—convey to your staff a clear vision of what you hope your organization, division, department, or team will achieve. Then enable your staff to live out that vision by helping them set goals, or *strategic imperatives*. Staff who understand where their organization is headed and what their role is, are far more motivated than staff who are left in the dark.

Focus Your Vision

Joy didn't know how to react to her promotion to manager. She was excited about the pay raise and the new responsibilities, and she knew more about her department than anyone. But she doubted her leadership ability. "I just don't have charisma," she said to herself as she looked in the mirror.

"How will I ever get anyone to listen to me?"

Many correctional supervisors and managers share Joy's concern. They worry that they will be unable to articulate a vision for their staff because they aren't outgoing or charismatic. But correctional supervisors and managers don't need the charm of a politician or the appeal of a movie star to inspire staff motivation. What they need is a *clear vision* of what they want their department or team to achieve and a commitment to conveying that vision.

Motivating Staff
- **Clear vision**
- **Commitment to conveying the vision**

What Is Your Vision?

Many correctional organizations have a vision or mission statement that describes their ultimate goals. If your organization has one, you might start there. Determine what your unit or department needs to do in order to live out its part of that vision. But, whether your organization has a vision statement or not, you can certainly articulate a vision for your team or department and convey it to your team. In fact, you should ask for your staff's input and invite them to brainstorm with you.

Your vision does not need to consider the specifics of how you will meet your goals—that comes later. What it needs to do is clearly define the results you hope your team or department will achieve in a way that will inspire your staff. After all, if you don't have a destination in mind, how will you and your staff know when you get there?

Try to sum up your vision in a single sentence. Here are a few examples, but don't let them limit your own creativity.

- For a word-processing department: Support management by completing all assignments on deadline, without errors.

- For a customer service department in prison industry: Provide superior service to customers by responding to all inquiries quickly and courteously.

Here are a few examples from departments of corrections.

The Illinois Department of Corrections defines its vision, or "mission statement" as the following:

"To protect the public from criminal offenders through a system of incarceration and supervision which securely segregates offenders from society, assures offenders of their constitutional rights, and maintains programs to enhance the success of the offenders' re-entry into society."

The Florida Department of Corrections defines its mission statement as the following:

"To protect the public, provide a safe and humane environment for staff and offenders, work in partnership with the community to provide programs and services to offenders, and supervise offenders at a level of security commensurate with the danger they present."

The New Hampshire Department of Corrections defines its mission statement as the following:

"To protect the public, offer offenders the opportunity for self-improvement, and promote staff development and personal growth in a safe environment."

Take a Moment . . .

Does your agency have a mission? If so, write it down.

____

____

____

____

What is your vision for your own division, department, unit or team? Take some time now to brainstorm. Then, try to sum up your visions in a sentence.

____

____

____

Set Strategic Imperatives

"Welcome to the facility," Carmen's new correctional manager said enthusiastically. "Our mission is to become the leading juvenile facility in the state. I know you'll work hard and do your part to make our facility great."

"Thank you," Carmen answered. "I've heard a lot about your organization's goals, and I think they're very exciting. But I was hoping you could tell me some specific things I can do to get started."

"Oh, I don't know; I'm not a detail person," the manager answered distractedly as she walked out the door. "Just look through the files; I'm sure you'll think of something."

Strategic Imperatives are limited, specific goals that we can complete and measure.

It's hard for staff to remain inspired when

they have no specific goals. Your organizational and departmental mission statements are good motivational starting points. But to maintain that motivation, you will need to set objectives, or *strategic imperatives*, for your department or unit and individual staff members. Strategic imperatives are limited, specific goals that we can complete and measure. For example, the facility security department whose vision is to become one of the top units in the state could set the strategic imperative of updating their security procedures.

Creating Strategic Imperatives

Each of your staff members should have individual strategic imperatives that will contribute to reaching your department's or team's overall vision. Get all of your staff members involved in the process—not only in creating their own goals but also in developing goals for the department. Your department's *overall goal* should already be evident or at least outlined by you. It never hurts to remind staff members of the goal(s) if you haven't done so lately.

Work with your staff to establish strategic imperatives that are tailored to their needs. Some staff members, especially those without a lot of work experience, may be intimidated by goals that appear too difficult. They can begin with more modest strategic imperatives that will build a string of small successes before they move on to bigger ones. Don't assign any staff members more goals than they can handle. Sure, you want to get the work done, but the formidable task of trying to get a huge number of projects completed can decrease motivation.

TIP: The longer a challenge has been around, the longer it will take to solve the problem. Plan accordingly when setting strategic imperatives related to such a problem. This will prevent your good workers from getting frustrated and your less-productive workers from giving up entirely.

Though you want to keep strategic imperatives manageable, leave room for those staff members who are habitual overachievers. Consider the following example:

> *Gloria worked in the finance department of a correctional agency. She not only achieved those goals set out by the finance director but also found new areas that needed to be explored. She put in a good deal of time on her extra projects and hoped that her willingness to take on extra work would be rewarded. But, though her supervisor acknowledged her extra efforts in her performance review, there was no other reward.*
>
> *Soon Gloria realized that extra work did not mean extra pay or anything else.* Why work so hard? *she thought. She began to accomplish only what was set out in her original goals and when she thought of new areas to tackle, she kept her mouth shut. After a few months, she decided to leave and start her own business. This wasn't part of her original career plan. She just thought it would be a good move because the traditional workplace had never valued her extra drive.*

People who willingly take on more work, like Gloria, are hard to come by—don't lose them! Support their ongoing motivation by making their goals expandable. Explain to staff that though there is a set list of strategic imperatives, if they see another item that needs to be included, by all means add it. Most importantly, reward them for their extra foresight and the extra work they do.

Give hard workers expandable goals.

Take a Moment . . .

Identify three staff members in your department or team and write their names below. What are strategic imperatives you could set for each that would help your department or team achieve its goals?

Name	Strategic Imperatives or Goals

Don't Forget the Positive

Too often, strategic imperatives are created to strengthen a weakness, as when organizations try to boost morale or improve communications. Don't limit yourself to the negative. You'll be able to generate more ideas when you base some of your goals on areas that are already successful. Plus, it's fulfilling for your staff to be reminded of the things they have done well.

Base some goals on successful areas.

As you and your staff develop strategic imperatives, view your work from dual perspectives. Notice that for each element, its opposite is included:

- What are our strengths, and how can we make them stronger?
- What are our weaknesses, and how can we be stronger in those areas?
- Who are our supporters, and how can they help us more?

- Who are our opponents, and how can we relate more effectively?
- What outside influences threaten our success, and how can we lessen the impact?
- What outside influences boost our success, and how can we be more successful?
- What inside influences threaten our success, and how can we be more successful?
- What inside influences boost our success and how can we be more successful?

Take a Moment . . .

How would you answer each question? Use extra paper if necessary.

What are our strengths, and how can we make them stronger?

____

____

What are our weaknesses, and how can we be stronger in those areas? ______________________________________

____

Who are our supporters, and how can they help us more?

____

____

Who are our opponents, and how can we relate more effectively?

____

____

What outside influences threaten our success, and how can we lessen the impact? ______________________________

____

What outside influences boost our success, and how can we be more successful? ______________________________

____

What inside influences boost our success and how can we be more successful? ______________________________

____

Measure Staff Progress

It was a beautiful spring afternoon, and Jerry could almost hear his favorite golf course calling his name. He knew that he was behind on his parolee calls and should make some calls, but he just didn't see any point. He couldn't remember the last time anyone had actually checked on his work. Why should he give up this beautiful afternoon when no one would even notice?

Your staff will be much more motivated to meet their strategic imperatives if they know that their work will be recognized. That means that you will need a way to measure their progress and achievements.

Creating Job Measures

Job measures provide a way to quantify staff progress in meeting their strategic imperatives. Your job measures should relate to the type of goals that you and a staff member have agreed upon. Some goals are easier to measure than others because they deal with things that can be easily counted. If, in the previous example, Jerry had a strategic imperative to raise his parolee calls by 20 percent, his correctional supervisor could measure his performance. Likewise, the correctional supervisor of a production worker can easily count the number of units that the worker produces in a given time period.

But some goals are not so easy to measure. How would you measure the performance of an office manager, a correctional officer, or a nurse? Here are a few variables you might consider:

- Timeliness—consider the number of times deadlines are met and the reasons why deadlines are missed.

- Accuracy—consider the staff member's ability to perform without error.
- Following procedures—consider the staff member's ability to follow standard procedures, such as the routine filing of reports.

Take a Moment . . . 

Think of a position in your department. What are some aspects of that position that you could measure?

____

____

____

____

Remember that you won't be able to measure every aspect of every job—some aspects of performance are difficult to quantify. Don't give up easily, however. Look for the processes that can be measured. When you run out of ideas, think some more, read, study, ask for advice, or go to a workshop.

To help staff get the most from job measurements, keep these guidelines in mind:

- Encourage staff members to see measurement as a way to promote self-growth, not as a way for you to check up on them.
- Communicate measurement results (goal achievement) when it will help to do so.
- Make sure that you are always measuring processes, and not assessing the value of people.

- Measure processes related to your own position too.

Develop an awareness of measurement within your facility or organization. This will take time if it hasn't been done before. Get staff members thinking about which tasks they can measure; how they can instigate self-improvement through measures; and how they can become involved in the process of improving quality.

TIP: Use measurement as a positive role-modeling device. Start a monthly quality review (if applicable for your organization), and each month, look for one staff member's effort that you can highlight. Find a specific tie-in. With some people this specific tie-in might be obvious. Vary whom you feature, however. A superstar worker can't be the focus each month, or this practice will discourage motivation in others. Remain positive. Don't use this mechanism to point out that others are doing less, aren't up to par, or aren't contributing.

Managing for Continuous Improvement

If your organization has a Continuous Improvement—Total Quality Management (TQM) program—in place, you will need to inspire ongoing staff motivation in order to make it effective.

If possible, begin improvement efforts with people who already have a strong level of motivation.

If possible, begin your quality efforts with staff members who already have a strong level of motivation. Workers with a low level of motivation may not be ready to deal with issues of quality on an ongoing basis. If they're having trouble caring about coming to work, they will have real trouble caring about creating a quality product or service.

Work with these staff members in a more basic way until you can understand what they need before you make a full-fledged push toward Continuous Improvement. This doesn't mean that you should ignore issues of quality completely. Rather, you should wait until some of the more basic issues are resolved before you begin discussing the fine points of Continuous Improvement or TQM.

TIP: People who have difficulty maintaining their motivation over a long period of time might not be suited for an organization practicing Continuous Improvement. Continuous Improvement, like its name sounds, is continuous—it never ends.

For staff who already have a strong level of motivation, Continuous Improvement can be an important part of their drive to help everyone succeed. Here are some guidelines to help you support staff motivation to maintain quality.

- **Emphasize that everyone is a link in the quality chain.** If one link breaks, the chain breaks. Help staff recognize that quality rests not only on the shoulders of the entire group but also on the shoulders of each person.
- **Allow each worker to overrule everyone when she or he knows something is not top quality.** *Quality* needs to be the ultimate authority.
- **Respect staff members' judgment and give them both accountability and authority.** Authority without accountability is dangerous. But together they provide the

ultimate support for responsibility and motivation.

- **Make results measurable and broadcast those results so that everyone can see progress.**
- **Make quality part of the process even when it's difficult.** The test of a true quality organization is its ability to maintain high standards under pressure.

Take a Moment . . .

Does your facility or organization currently have a Continuous Improvement or Total Quality Management program? If so, how do staff respond to it? Can you think of anything management can do to improve staff response? List your ideas below:

If your facility or organization doesn't have a Continuous Improvement program in place, how do you think staff would react if one were started? What could management do to inspire staff to accept such a program?

Base Leadership on Values

You might remember that the *Industry Week* survey quoted earlier stated that staff were inspired by leaders with vision and *values*. To fully inspire your vision for your team, the way you treat staff must be grounded in a set of values that they respect.

The term *values* means different things to different people. You and your staff probably do not share all the same values, nor should you expect to. However, there are some basic values shared by many people that can be particularly inspiring in the workplace. These include:

- **Respect for others**—All of your efforts to inspire motivation will be useless if you don't treat your staff with respect. You can set an example by treating those outside your department with consideration as well.
- **Honesty and integrity**—As our society becomes more and more disillusioned, honesty and integrity in leadership are increasingly valued. Your staff want to know that they can trust you. They also want to know that you do what you say you are going to do whether you're dealing with other staff members or offenders.
- **Fairness**—We've all heard horror stories of the slacker who's promoted over the hardworking staff member because he's the boss's friend. Though the example is exaggerated, nothing can decrease motivation faster than the perception of unfairness. Avoid favoritism when dealing with staff members or offenders, and be sure that your staff understand the basis for your decisions.

These are just a few of the values that can inspire motivation in your staff. Though they may seem basic, they can make the difference between staff who approach their jobs, co-workers, and offenders with cynicism—and those who are inspired to put forth their very best efforts. Staff who are treated with respect, honesty, and fairness will return that loyalty to their organization and reflect it when dealing with others.

Take a Moment . . . 

Are there other values that you think are important in the workplace? Add them to the list of values below.

Value	**Action**
Respect for others	______________________________
	______________________________
Honesty and Integrity	______________________________
	______________________________
Fairness	______________________________
	______________________________

Describe actions correctional supervisors and managers can take to live out these values when dealing with staff.

____

____

____

____

Maintain Your Vision

Inspiring staff vision doesn't require personal charisma or a dynamic personality. What it does require is the ability to:

- Imagine the results you want your department or team to achieve.
- Identify strategic imperatives that will help your department or team

meet those results.

- Determine how to measure staff progress.
- Maintain quality.
- Live out good workplace values.

Staff who understand their organization's mission and their role in it maintain motivation better than staff who are left in the dark. In our next chapter, we'll consider how you can continue to inspire motivation by rewarding staff for a job well done.

Your challenge as a correctional supervisor or manager is to convey to your staff a clear vision of what you hope your department or team will achieve.

Summary

The number one factor that inspires staff motivation is vision. Your challenge as a correctional supervisor or manager is to convey to your staff a clear vision of what you hope your department or team will achieve. You can begin to develop a department vision by examining your organization's overall vision or mission statement. Your vision does not need to consider the specifics of how you will meet your goals. It does, however, need to articulate the *results* you hope your department or team will achieve in a way that will inspire your staff.

To remain inspired by your vision, your staff need strategic imperatives that will help them live out that vision. *Strategic imperatives* are limited, specific goals that staff can complete and measure. You should develop strategic imperatives for your department as a whole and for individual staff. Tailor imperatives for individual staff members to their specific needs and involve them in the goal-setting process. As you create the goals, focus on what your department is currently doing well—as well as what needs improvement.

Maintain staff motivation to meet strategic imperatives by monitoring staff progress. Use job measures to quantify staff progress in meeting their strategic imperatives. Some strategic imperatives are easier to measure than others because they deal with things that can be counted. Others are more difficult. To measure them, you might want to consider such variables as time lines, accuracy, and following procedures.

If your organization has a Continuous Improvement or Total Quality Management program in place, you will need to inspire ongoing staff motivation to make it effective. It's best to begin quality efforts with staff who already have a strong level of motivation—less motivated staff members need more basic work before they're ready for the fine points of Continuous Improvement. When you do begin quality efforts with your staff, follow these guidelines to inspire and maintain staff motivation:

- Emphasize that everyone is a link in the quality chain.
- Allow each staff member to overrule everyone when she or he knows something is not top quality.
- Respect staff judgment; give them both accountability and authority.
- Make results measurable and broadcast those results so that everyone can see progress.
- Make quality part of the process even when it's difficult.

Finally, remember that staff are inspired by values as well as vision. Practicing values—such as respect for others, honesty, and fairness—will inspire staff. It also encourages staff to use the same values when dealing with co-workers and offenders.

Chapter Three Review

Answers to these questions appear on pages 110–111.

1. What does a vision or mission statement do? ________________

   ____

2. What are strategic imperatives?

   ____

   ____

3. What do job measures do?

   ____

   ____

4. Below you will find the guidelines for maintaining staff motivation for a quality program. Fill in the missing words.

   A. Emphasize that everyone is a ______ in the quality chain.

   B. Allow each staff member to _______ everyone when she or he knows that something is not top quality.

   C. Give staff authority, and hold them ___________for every decision.

   D. Make results ___________ and broadcast those results so that everyone can see progress.

   E. Make ___________ part of the process even when it's difficult.

5. What are three values that can inspire staff? ________________

   ____

   ____

Chapter Four

REWARDING YOUR STAFF

Chapter Objectives

After completing this chapter, you should be able to:

- Identify the rewards that your staff value.
- Distribute rewards fairly.
- Use recognition rewards effectively.
- Explain how to keep rewards from backfiring.

What gets rewarded gets done. This statement is true, but a bit too simple. Rewards can inspire staff motivation, but only if correctional supervisors and managers match the right reward to the right staff member. A poorly planned reward system may do nothing to encourage staff motivation, or at worst, may actually discourage it.

To motivate your staff, you need to match the right reward to the right staff member.

To ensure that rewards work to *support* motivation instead of hinder it, correctional supervisors and managers need to understand:

- the relationship between rewards and motivation and
- the features of an effective reward system.

Inspire Motivation Through Rewards

There are many different types of rewards. In the corrections workplace, rewards typically include promotions, job titles, better offices and praise from supervisors or peers.

To motivate your staff, you need to match the right reward to the right staff member. If all rewards could inspire motivation in all staff members, your job as a correctional supervisor or manager would be easy—simply offer any reward and watch motivation skyrocket. But rewards can be tricky. Sometimes they succeed in inspiring staff motivation, and sometimes they don't, as in the examples that follow:

> *Juanita loves praise and appreciates a compliment more than any other type of reward. When she is praised by her supervisor or co-workers, she practically bounces around the office! The next time she's asked to do a certain task, she does it even more enthusiastically than before, remembering her past positive experiences.*
>
> *Terry, on the other hand, has trouble accepting compliments. He's a dedicated worker who maintains high standards of quality. But when praised for a job well done, he's actually a little embarrassed. His inner thoughts are, "I just got lucky this time."*

In our first example, praise inspired the staff motivation the supervisor hoped for. In our second example, though, the praise actually created a negative response—there was no support for motivation. Terry's supervisor would have received a better response if he had offered Terry some other type of reward—heading a committee, taking the lead on an important project, asking for his ideas about a new procedure. The contrast between the two staff members points out the importance of creating a reward system that offers the right reward to the right worker.

Take a Moment . . .

Think of those you supervise. Can you identify which types of rewards are most likely to inspire a positive response? List them below. Keep in mind that few people, if any, are motivated solely by one type of reward. Look for which of the two types is likely to be the best motivator.

Name	Reward Type
____________	______________
____________	______________
____________	______________
____________	______________

Choose Rewards Carefully

As we saw in the previous example, there is no guarantee that the reward you offer will inspire motivation. However, there are some things you can do to make it more likely that your staff will react favorably to the rewards you offer. Generally, staff are more likely to react favorably to a reward if:

- They value the reward and see the reward as worth the effort it will take to earn it.
- They understand how to earn the reward; the reward is clearly linked to specific behaviors.
- They see the reward as attainable; the performance level necessary is reachable.
- They see the reward system as fair.

Offer a Reward the Staff Member Values

"If we successfully open the new facility by our timeline, you'll all get a great reward!" Burton announced to his staff. "Can't tell you what it is yet—it's a surprise!"

Dreaming of a sizable cash bonus that would pay off her credit cards, Mason worked hard. During breaks, she and other staff members gossiped about what the reward might be. But after a few days, the excited chatter in the break room turned sour.

"I want to know what the reward is," Mason's friend Hanson complained. "I've never worked so hard in my life, and all we might be getting is a certificate of thanks."

The questions were so frequent that Burton finally revealed the reward: If the goal was met, staff members would have the opportunity to travel to a week-long training program of their choice. All expenses would be paid!

Mason immediately lost her motivation to meet the goal. Why?

1. She didn't really want to participate in any of the training programs offered in the catalog.
2. She was a single mother of twin preschool boys. Getting a baby-sitter would be tough, and she didn't want to leave her children for a full week.
3. She sure as heck didn't want to spend her time being trained when she'd rather be on vacation with her kids.

In the following weeks, Mason learned that several of her co-workers had similar reactions. She wasn't surprised when the timeline wasn't met.

Though Mason wasn't surprised when the goal wasn't met, her supervisor undoubtedly was. But Burton should never have assumed that all of his staff members would place the same value on his offer.

As this example illustrates, people's reactions to rewards vary according to their life circumstances and individual preferences. When staff members don't value a reward, they won't be motivated to make the effort to earn it. Offering an incentive to his staff without knowing their preferences backfired for Burton. He should have done some homework to learn what types of rewards his staff valued.

People's reactions to rewards vary according to their life circumstances and individual preferences.

Take a Moment . . .

List below which types of rewards inspire you.

____

____

How do your rewards— what you value— differ from those you identified for your staff on page 46?

Though your staff shouldn't dictate every aspect of a reward system, you should certainly take their needs and desires into account. You can develop some understanding of their preferences simply by visiting with them in the break room or other informal settings. You can also learn about them through more formal situations, such as performance appraisals or departmental meetings. You might even consider asking staff to fill out a survey, such as the one on the following page.

Take a Moment . . .

I would like (check one of the three):

Job Element	More	Less	Currently Okay
Praise	____	____	____
Supervision	____	____	____
Direction	____	____	____
Being on a team	____	____	____
Leading a team	____	____	____
Goals	____	____	____
Structure	____	____	____
Chance for promotion	____	____	____
Chance for education/ training	____	____	____
Flexibility of workplace	____	____	____
Flexibility of work time	____	____	____
Decision making	____	____	____
Workload	____	____	____
Meetings	____	____	____
Responsibility	____	____	____
Recognition	____	____	____
Respect	____	____	____
Freedom of expression	____	____	____
Awards	____	____	____
Salary	____	____	____
Vacation	____	____	____
Personal days	____	____	____

You may not be able to give your staff some of these items at this time. Keep them on the list anyway. For example, suppose you find that your entire staff wants more personal days. Then perhaps you can begin to influence the facility structure so that they eventually can be provided. At the very least, you can pass the suggestion on to *your* supervisor.

You might try giving staff two copies of the survey. Ask them to fill out one copy to reflect what they would like to receive from you. Have them complete the other to reflect what they would like to receive from their peers. Items such as "salary" that cannot be provided by peers could be designated N/A (not applicable).

Clearly Explain How to Earn the Reward

Ivan had worked at the correctional facility for two years, and he'd never been named Employee of the Month. Many of the other correctional officers had seen their photos posted on the special bulletin board. They had been allowed to park in the special Employee of the Month parking space, but he was always left out. Finally, he decided to ask his supervisor.

"I've always wondered why I've never been named Employee of the Month," Ivan said to his supervisor one afternoon. "Could you tell me what I'd have to do to be considered?"

"Work a lot harder than you do now, that's what," the supervisor said.

Staff must know how to earn rewards.

A reward won't inspire a staff member if the person doesn't know how to earn it. As a correctional supervisor or manager, you must establish the performance level to be achieved in a specific way. Simply telling someone to "do better" isn't good enough. A staff member must be given a precise goal.

If you have difficulty setting specific goals for your staff, review the previous chapter, especially the section on job measures. Some achievements can be difficult to measure numerically, but even if you can't translate a task into numbers, it is possible to get specific. For example, Ivan's supervisor might have talked about whether Ivan arrived at work on time, was able to fill in for other officers without errors, wrote reports correctly, conducted searches properly, and so forth.

Officer Tyler was anxious to get a new shift. He knew that receiving such a reward, however, would not be easy. He had received low ratings in several areas on a recent performance evaluation.

Tyler's supervisor told him that he could earn his way to a new shift. During the next 30 days, Tyler would have to make no errors in any area of his performance. This meant arriving at work on time, completing all his tasks to perfection, and having no adverse incidents with co-workers. Tyler left his supervisor's office excited about the possibility of getting on a new shift.

Over the next few days, Tyler worked exceptionally hard. But he became stressed and overwhelmed trying to avoid making mistakes. He could get only so much help from his fellow officers. The truth was, he needed to improve in more than these areas, and he couldn't make the changes all at once.

Tyler soon gave up his effort to "be perfect" for 30 days. He returned to doing the best he could, which meant struggling with many of his tasks. This example is extreme, but it proves a point.

Be Sure That the Reward Is Attainable

An unattainable reward can turn against itself.

This attempt to inspire motivation suffered because the staff member didn't perceive the reward as being attainable. People aren't motivated by a reward unless they believe they can reach the performance level required to earn it. As Tyler's story illustrates, an unattainable reward can turn against itself. Staff members can become bitter or resentful when they perceive a reward as impossible to achieve. Eventually, they may begin to doubt their overall abilities.

Correctional supervisors and managers walk a fine line in determining the level of performance to be rewarded. On one hand, the goal must be high enough to present a challenge to the staff member, or else the reward will be meaningless. On the other hand, the performance level cannot be so high that the staff member sees it as unreasonable or impossible.

In Tyler's case, his supervisor knew that the facility would benefit if Tyler could improve his performance—especially if he achieved a high rating in each performance area. But the supervisor gave little thought to Tyler's actual ability to do it given his time and resource limits. Instead, the supervisor thought, "Why not offer that carrot-on-a-stick? If Tyler can't achieve it, we have nothing to lose." But the facility had something BIG to lose—Tyler's motivation.

Take a Moment . . .

Has there been a time when you wanted a particular reward and couldn't get it? How did it affect you? Jot down your thoughts below.

Reward:

Performance required to get the reward:

Personal belief level that the award could be earned: 0 = No belief; 5 = Total confidence

Ratings

Circle one:

0 1 2 3 4 5

Think about a similar situation involving someone you know. How did it affect that person? Describe what happened:

Establish a Fair Reward System

Greta tore eagerly at her pay envelope. Her check with the latest raise was inside. Steve had bragged all month about the new stereo system he was buying with his raise. She'd worked just as hard as he had, and she had plenty of uses for the extra money. But when she saw the amount of her check, her anticipation changed to anger. This raise couldn't be anywhere near what Steve had gotten—why was there such a difference?

"I wonder if it's because I'm a woman?" Greta asked herself. If that was the case, what was the use of putting out her best effort? No matter what she did, she'd never get ahead.

To inspire motivation in your staff, your reward must be equitable.

To inspire motivation in all your staff, your reward system must be equitable. Both Steve and Greta should get the same raise or it spells trouble—and in this case, possible charges of discrimination. Though this point might seem obvious, remember that reward systems can become skewed because of the supervisor's perception of various staff members.

Suppose that you decide to reward your staff for reaching their performance goals. You feel certain that your cooperative, friendly staff members—José, Sandra, and Bill—will achieve it. But Ryan, who is on probation for tardiness, and whom you suspect has a drinking problem, achieves the goal first. Would you be tempted to give Ryan less than the others because he's on probation? Some supervisors would. But ask yourself what this would do to the equity of the reward system—and to Ryan's motivation. If there's no consistency in your rewards, the whole system could fall apart.

Following the guidelines discussed will help you establish an effective reward system for your staff. Next, we'll consider how to use the most common type of reward available for correctional staff: *recognition*.

Take a Moment . . .

Review the last reward that you offered your staff. Did it follow all four of the guidelines we just discussed? Check them off on the list below:

______ The staff valued the reward and saw the reward as worth the effort it took to earn it.

______ The staff understood how to earn the reward; the reward was clearly linked to specific behaviors.

______ The staff saw the reward as attainable; the performance level necessary was reachable.

______ The staff saw the reward system as fair.

Did your reward system work? Why or why not? If you didn't follow all of the guidelines, list the ones you missed and note how leaving them out affected the plan.

Reward with Recognition

Recognition rewards can inspire motivation by showing staff that their hard work is noticed and appreciated.

There are many types of rewards that do not involve money or other material incentives, such as a bigger office. Recognition rewards can inspire motivation by showing staff that their hard work is noticed and appreciated. Some common types of recognition rewards include:

Giving staff more responsibility and decision-making authority. You don't need to give a staff member a formal promotion to empower that person with more responsibility and authority. Many staff members crave more control over their own work projects and would enjoy the chance to serve as a team facilitator or group leader. Identify those staff members and give them the chance to grow—and be sure they understand that with responsibility comes accountability.

TIP: Giving someone added responsibility does not mean just throwing more work at them. Be sure that your assignments are reasonable and that the staff member will find the new responsibility truly challenging, instead of more of the same old routine.

Recognizing a staff member publicly. Many staff members enjoy having their achievements recognized publicly. The acknowledgment can be as simple as briefly mentioning the staff member's accomplishment during a staff meeting or briefing.

Or your efforts can be more involved, such as giving the staff member a plaque or taking him or her to lunch.

TIP: Some staff members are shy or come from cultures in which public recognition is not considered appropriate. Get to know the members of your team and their preferences about public recognition. If you are unsure, ASK. If a staff member doesn't care for public recognition, don't forget to acknowledge her or his achievements privately.

Instituting a formal recognition program. Reward outstanding achievement by starting a formal reward program that recognizes outstanding achievement on a regular basis. Many organizations have Employee of the Month programs. If your organization does not have one, ask your supervisor about starting one—for the organization or your team.

TIP: If you do institute a formal recognition program, be sure that your staff understand the level of performance necessary to be recognized. Stress that all staff are capable of achieving recognition. Keep an eye out for staff members' successes so that you will be able to vary the individuals recognized. Recognizing the same two or three people month after month can discourage the motivation of other staff.

Praising a staff member informally. Don't wait for a performance evaluation to tell your staff they're doing a good job. Look for good performance and praise it regularly. Use praise to build morale and support motivation by following these guidelines:

Don't wait for a performance evaluation to tell your staff they're doing a good job.

- *Focus praise on performance, not personal qualities.* You may have many different reactions to the appearance and personality of your individual staff members. But your role as a correctional supervisor or manager is to focus on staff's actions when performing their jobs. Rather than complimenting Floyd on his new car, praise his ability to handle offender movement quickly and efficiently.

- *Make praise authentic.* Don't give praise unless you truly mean it. But when you see performance that deserves praise, be sure to give it.
- *Ensure that praise comes often enough to keep up morale, but not so often that it is expected.* This is a tough call. If someone is performing especially well, do you slow down your praise because you feel you're giving too many compliments too often? Not if your praise is authentic. Just don't make your praise a rigid routine, such as one compliment per day, per staff member. If staff realize they're receiving the *Compliment du Jour* (Compliment of the Day), the praise won't have as much inherent value.
- *Understand how praise affects each individual that you supervise.* Some people enjoy receiving praise so much that they prefer it over a letter of commendation. Some people are so shy that they are embarrassed even by private praise. Some people value other recognition, such as increased decision-making power and responsibility, more than praise. Identify people for whom praise is not effective. Then look for other types of recognition that can motivate them.

Take a Moment . . .

Are you using praise as effectively as you could? Write "Yes" or "No" next to the following guidelines:

Do you . . .

______ Give praise when it's deserved?

______ Make certain that praise is authentic?

______ Ensure that praise comes often enough to keep up morale but not so often that it is expected?

______ Understand how praise affects each individual you supervise?

Based on your answers, what could you do to make your use of praise more effective?

____

____

____

____

____

List the types of recognition that you can give your staff members. Identify staff members who deserve a reward—be sure to explain why.

____

____

____

____

Don't Let Rewards Backfire

As you decide what rewards to offer your staff, keep in mind that some rewards can have negative as well as positive consequences. When you reward the achievement of some staff—with a nice office, or a reserved parking space—you run the risk of alienating staff who believe that they, too, should be rewarded.

Some rewards can have negative as well as positive consequences.

There is no way to eliminate feelings of jealousy on the part of your staff. But you *can* reduce that negative emotion by following these simple guidelines.

Be as fair as possible in your distribution of rewards. Be sure that those singled out for rewards fully deserve them. Most staff recognize a hard worker and will not resent the person being rewarded.

Monitor staff performance and recognize hard work on the part of all staff members. Most staff will not resent the recognition of others if their work is recognized too. This does not mean that you must give every staff a certificate on a regular basis. But it does mean that you should acknowledge their successes as often as possible.

Find ways to recognize smaller accomplishments as well as larger ones. Not everyone will win the Employee of the Month award. How can you recognize those who work consistently with good results?

Set reasonable performance standards for rewards, and regularly let all staff know how they can reach them. Staff must believe that their own work is appreciated and that they have a chance to meet performance standards. Only then will they be much more likely to celebrate other staff accomplishments instead of resenting them.

Take a Moment . . .

Is your organization doing all it can to distribute rewards fairly? Using the guidelines from the previous page, identify ways in which your organization deals effectively with rewards and areas in which it could use improvement.

Effective Use of Rewards

Areas That Need Improvement

How can you recommend improvements to your supervisor?

Summary

Rewards can inspire staff motivation, but only if correctional supervisors and managers match the right reward to the right worker. Generally, staff are more likely to react favorably to a reward if:

- They value the reward and see the reward as worth the effort it will take to earn it.
- They understand how to earn the reward; the reward is clearly linked to specific behaviors.
- They see the reward as attainable; the performance level necessary is reachable.
- They see the reward system as fair.

One of the most basic ways that correctional supervisors and managers reward staff is with recognition rewards that show appreciation for good performance. Recognition rewards can inspire motivation by showing staff that their hard work is noticed and appreciated.

Some common types of recognition rewards include:

- Giving a staff member more responsibility and decision-making authority.
- Recognizing a staff member publicly.
- Instituting a formal recognition program.
- Praising a staff member informally.

Your praise of a staff member's performance will be most effective if you:

- Focus praise on performance, not personal qualities.
- Make praise authentic.

- Ensure that praise comes often enough to keep up morale but not so often that it is expected.
- Understand how praise affects each individual whom you supervise.

Whenever you single out some staff members for rewards, you run the risk that other staff members will be jealous. There is no way to totally eliminate feelings of jealousy on the part of your staff. But you can reduce that negative emotion by following these simple guidelines:

- Be as fair as possible in your distribution of rewards.
- Monitor staff performance and recognize hard work on the part of all staff.
- Find ways to recognize smaller accomplishments as well as larger ones.
- Set reasonable performance standards for rewards, and regularly let all staff know how they can reach them.

Rewarding your staff's good performance lets them know that you notice their efforts and appreciate them, which can inspire motivation. But rewards are not the only means of inspiring staff motivation. In our next chapter, we'll consider how maintaining a positive work environment can also support and encourage motivation.

Chapter Four Review

Answers to these questions appear on pages 111–112.

1. A ___________ can be effective only if the staff member values what is being offered.

2. A staff member must see a reward as _______________ for it to be effective.

3. Which type of reward can inspire motivation by showing staff that their hard work is noticed and appreciated?

   A. Recognition
   B. Monetary
   C. Attainable
   D. All of the above

4. True/False. Praising staff is important. If you can't find anything to praise about their performance, compliment them on their appearance.

5. List four things you can do to keep rewards from backfiring.

   A. ____

   B. ____

   C. ____

   D. ____

Chapter Five

MAINTAINING A POSITIVE WORK ENVIRONMENT

Chapter Objectives

After completing this chapter, you should be able to:

- Describe positive reinforcement and negative reinforcement or, punishment.
- Use positive rather than negative reinforcement.
- Create a friendly work culture or environment.

Unlike the independently wealthy, most of us have to work in order to survive. But as we saw in Chapter Two, we also work because we want to. We find that many of our emotional and psychological needs are filled through our work, and we enjoy our jobs.

Staff need to feel respected and empowered.

As a correctional supervisor or manager, you can help staff want to come to work and help support their motivation. How can you do this, even with limited resources? You need to create a work environment in which staff feel respected and empowered. Two techniques that can help you create this type of positive work environment include:

- Emphasizing positive reinforcement
- Creating a friendly work culture

Emphasize Positive Reinforcement

Many of our ideas about reinforcement come from the work of B.F. Skinner. Skinner studied the ways in which animal behavior could be influenced by reinforcement. He identified three basic types of reinforcement:

- Positive reinforcement
- Negative reinforcement
- Punishment

People are not animals. But these types of reinforcement have numerous applications to human behavior and are often used by correctional supervisors and managers in the workplace.

Correctional supervisors and managers give *positive reinforcement* when they reward positive staff behavior with a positive response. The positive response may take many forms, such as praise or public recognition. A correctional supervisor or manager might offer positive reinforcement by saying something like, "If you keep working overtime to help us out, you'll be in line for the next promotion."

Correctional supervisors and managers give *negative reinforcement* when they encourage positive staff behavior by not carrying through on a negative response. This type of reinforcement is similar to a threat; the negative response may be fairly serious, such as a lost job or demotion, or relatively minor, such as a wrist-slapping from the supervisor. A correctional supervisor or manager might offer negative reinforcement by saying something like, "I'm tired of you coming in late. If you keep this up, you'll lose your job." By coming in on time, the employee avoids the negative consequence of being fired.

Take a Moment . . .

To examine just how damaging negative reinforcement is, think back on your own early experiences with negative reinforcement.

1. What is your first memory of negative reinforcement?

   Did it work? Why or why not?

2. How did it make you feel about the person issuing the demand?

3. What was your worst school-age experience with negative reinforcement?

4. Which teachers motivated with negative reinforcement, and what threats did they use?

5. Have you experienced negative reinforcement at work? If so, how did it affect you and your job performance?

6. Have you used negative reinforcement in dealing with staff? What was the cause—anger, impatience, inability to think of another approach?

7. What were the short-term and long-term effects of negative reinforcement? (Be honest when answering this last question. Temporary improvements in job performance can mask feelings of resentment, distrust, and fear created by negative reinforcement.) Do you know how your staff really feel?

Correctional supervisors and managers use punishment when they meet negative behavior with a negative response. As with negative reinforcement, the punishment may take many forms, with varying degrees of severity. However, with punishment, the negative response is carried through—usually immediately. A supervisor might offer punishment by saying something like, "You're either absent or late far too much to be of value to this agency so I'm putting you on administrative leave."

Punishment means to penalize and cause pain, loss or suffering for a wrongdoing. The purpose is to impose a consequence for the person who broke the rule. The idea behind punishment is that, hopefully, the rulebreaker will remember the pain and follow the rule in the future. It produces short-term results at best. The person punished may break the rule again when you're not around. At the very least, the work environment probably would not be positive.

Unlike punishment, discipline means to educate, train or instruct. The root word of discipline is "disciple." Disciples are learners. You are the teacher—your staff are the learners. The purpose of discipline is to teach a person a new way of thinking or behaving. Discipline not only tells a staff member what behavior to stop but what behavior to *begin*. The staff member learns that he or she has a choice in how to behave.

For example, instead of threatening a staff member for not making log entries, you discipline him. True, it will require more patience and time on your part. You must sit down with him and work through the disciplinary process. But by doing so, you will be conveying respect for the staff member and explaining the positive behavior he must start—making proper log entries. In the long run, your time and effort will result in a positive work environment and, hopefully, a long term behavior change for the staff member.

The chart below summarizes the differences between punishment and discipline.

PUNISHMENT	DISCIPLINE
Intent is to penalize	Intent is to teach
Emphasis is on power or authority	Emphasis is on respect for others
Implies moral judgment; doer of deed is bad	Treats person with dignity; separates deed from doer
Involves overt or covert threats of disrespect or violence	Involves use of calm voice and communicates respect
Demands compliance	Presents choices for the future

So, when a situation calls for discipline—such as a staff member who has broken facility rules, is habitually late, or harasses other staff—follow your facility disciplinary policies and procedures. Avoid the temptation to punish the individual by yelling at him or threatening him. Remember that your goal is a long-term change in behavior and a positive work environment.

Take a Moment . . .

Identify which statements are examples of positive reinforcement (PR), negative reinforcement (NR), and punishment (P). Answers are given on page 112.

______ 1. "Those boxes need to be loaded on the truck in the next hour, or you'll have some explaining to do."

______ 2. "I want to recognize Jacqueline for the wonderful job she did preparing a totally new schedule for the department."

______ 3. "Randy, you continue to come to work late—this is the third time in two weeks! I'm putting you on probation."

______ 4. "If you make this many errors on your next report, I'll have to put a note in your personnel file."

Negative reinforcement and punishment can build a workplace climate of fear and distrust.

If you've been a correctional supervisor or manager for any length of time, you've probably used negative reinforcement and punishment on at least a few occasions. Use of negative reinforcement can be especially tempting because some threats can lead to improved staff performance in the short term. But in the long run, repeated use of negative reinforcement and punishment can lead to serious problems. These methods can build a workplace climate of fear or anger and distrust. Staff may feel that their job security is constantly threatened. Such feelings are bound to discourage staff motivation.

Note: While punishment is not an effective means of *encouraging* staff performance either, there may be times when you will need to discipline staff, such as those who

- have broken organizational rules,
- are habitually late, or
- harass other staff.

When this occurs, use your organization's official disciplinary channels.

Supporting good performance through positive reinforcement is a more effective way of letting staff know the level of job performance you expect. Even a staff member who is having trouble on the job must have one or two small successes. Point these out and talk with the person about how she or he can extend the same level of performance to other aspects of the job.

Choose the Right Positive Reinforcement

Knowing which type of reward to offer to which staff member is an important part of using positive reinforcement effectively. We've already seen that individual staff members can react quite differently to praise and public recognition. The only way you can learn what type of positive reinforcement to offer your staff is to get to know them as individuals. Then you can reinforce from a position of strength rather than guessing wildly. Plus, getting to know your staff usually means spending more time with them, which in itself is a form of positive reinforcement.

Getting to know your staff in itself is a form of positive reinforcement.

One word of caution: As you get acquainted with your staff, don't become so carried away that your efforts start to resemble a full-scale investigation into their private lives. Your job as a correctional supervisor or manager is to discover your staffs' professional goals and to learn what rewards inspire motivation and good performance—not to pry into personal issues.

Create a Friendly Organizational Culture

A worker-friendly organization can inspire both motivation and organizational loyalty.

Besides positively reinforcing staff members on an individual level, you can also build goodwill at the group level. Create an organizational culture that's friendly to staff. A worker-friendly organization can inspire both motivation and organizational loyalty.

Every organization has its own unique culture, with much of it dictated by policies and procedures. However you characterize your organizational culture, there are things you and other correctional supervisors and managers can do to make that culture friendly toward staff, including:

- Offering opportunities for education and training.
- Offering flexibility to deal with family issues.
- Respecting the diversity of your staff.
- Accommodating physically challenged staff members (when appropriate).
- Providing opportunities to socialize outside work.

Offer Opportunities for Education and Training

Offering training to staff shows you value them.

Nothing can discourage motivation quicker than being told to complete a task you have no idea how to perform. This type of situation has become increasingly common as the workplace becomes more technologically advanced. How many staff members have found computers sitting on their desks that they have no idea how to use properly?

When your organization offers training to staff, it tells them that it values them and wants to make an investment in their future. Staff who feel confident in their skills will enjoy their work more and become greater assets to their organization.

Offer Flexibility to Deal with Family Issues

It's hard to concentrate on a job when you have a sick child at home or an aging parent facing surgery. Correctional organizations are increasing ways to help staff deal with family responsibilities and emergencies. Some alternatives you might consider include:

- Offering flex-time or changing a schedule so that parents can divide child-care duties.
- Providing staff with personal days to deal with family issues.

Giving your staff the flexibility to deal with family issues can help reduce staff turnover. It also shows that your organization cares about them as human beings as well as staff members.

Take a Moment . . .

What are some things your organization currently does to help staff meet the needs of their families?

What other things could your organization offer to help staff meet family needs?

What type of education and training does your facility or agency offer staff?

What other type of education and training could you offer?

What education and training resources could you offer staff (e.g., organizations, mentoring programs)?

Respect the Diversity of Your Workforce

As American society becomes increasingly diverse, that diversity is reflected in the workplace. Now, more than ever before, people from a variety of different ethnic groups, faiths, and socioeconomic backgrounds are asked to work together.

Staff from diverse backgrounds appreciate a supervisor who respects their diversity.

Staff from diverse backgrounds appreciate a supervisor who respects their diversity and expects all members of the organization to do the same. Be sure that all of your staff understand that harassment and discrimination will not be tolerated in your workplace. Remind staff that they may not all share the same religious holidays. Give staff the opportunity to get to know and appreciate aspects of each other's cultures.

Accommodate Physically Challenged Staff

Accommodating physically challenged staff isn't just a nice thing to do. Under the Americans with Disabilities Act, it's the law. Help your organization do whatever it can to adapt to the needs of the differently abled. Help all staff members judge co-workers on the basis of their abilities, not their disabilities—whether physical or not.

Provide Opportunities to Socialize

Work is more enjoyable when you like the people you work with. Your chance of liking them increases with the amount of social time you spend together.

Your chance of liking the people you work with increases with the amount of social time you spend together.

There are several ways to get staff together outside the workplace besides the annual facility barbecue. Regular group outings at sports and entertainment events and impromptu get-togethers after work are just a few ways you can unify people.

You can also build small social gatherings into the workday—special lunches, on-site gatherings for special events, etc. All organizational activities should be handled carefully so that they are appropriate, legal, and inclusive.

Be creative as you think of ways to brighten your organizational culture. Some facilities have special tee shirts and hats to show their pride in their organization. Others proudly display their accreditation certificate.

To develop more ideas for organizational social opportunities, list the following:

- Activities your organization currently conducts
- Social activities you've enjoyed with co-workers in past jobs
- People who would be good at managing after work activities
- Costs involved in launching new activities

In many correctional organizations, employee clubs can take the lead in organizing social events. Don't work in a vacuum. If you don't have an Employee Club, invite staff from across the organization to share their ideas for social activities. Sharing those ideas could become a social activity in itself.

Take a Moment . . .

Brainstorm some initial ideas for opportunities for organizational social events:

Activities we currently have in place:

New events we could try:

Create a Positive Work Environment

Positive reinforcement and a worker-friendly organizational culture are two factors that can create a positive work environment. When a work environment is pleasant, staff will enjoy coming to work, and they will be motivated to do their best. They will also feel loyalty to their organization, which will result in less staff turnover.

Take a Moment . . .

To help create a positive work environment, answer these questions:

What are some things you can do to create a positive work environment?

How can you get your staff involved in developing a positive work environment?

Which of your staff might be good at managing social activities?

Summary

As a correctional supervisor or manager, you can help staff want to come to work and help support their motivation. You can do this by creating a work environment in which staff feel respected and empowered. Two techniques that can help you create this type of positive work environment include:

- Emphasizing positive reinforcement
- Creating a friendly organizational or work culture

Many of our ideas about reinforcement come from the work of B.F. Skinner. He identified three basic types of reinforcement:

- **Positive reinforcement**—rewarding positive behavior with a positive response: "If you keep working overtime to help us out, you'll be in line for the next promotion."
- **Negative reinforcement**—rewarding positive behavior by not carrying through on a negative response: *"I'm tired of you coming in late and being absent—if you keep this up, you'll lose your job."* The person complies and avoids the negative response.
- **Punishment**—meeting negative behavior with a negative response: *"You're either late or absent far too much to be of value to this agency, so I'm putting you on administrative leave."*

Negative reinforcement may encourage improved staff performance in the short run. But in the long term, both negative reinforcement—and punishment—can discourage staff motivation by creating a workplace climate of fear, anger, and mistrust. Positive reinforcement is a more effective way of letting staff know your expectations. It creates a positive workplace that supports staff motivation.

Because individual staff members react differently to various types of positive reinforcement, correctional supervisors and managers need to tailor their reinforcement. They must give the right reinforcement to the right employee. To do this, they must get to know their staff members and their individual preferences.

Creating an organizational culture that is friendly toward staff also encourages strong motivation. Some ways you can do this include:

- Offering opportunities for education and training.
- Offering flexibility to deal with family issues.
- Respecting the diversity of your workforce.
- Accommodating physically challenged staff (when appropriate).
- Providing opportunities to socialize outside work.

Chapter Five Review

Answers to these questions appear on pages 112–113.

1. Match the following terms to the appropriate definition.

   ____ Positive reinforcement

   ____ Negative reinforcement

   ____ Punishment

   A. Rewarding positive behavior by not carrying through on a negative response

   B. Meeting negative behavior with a negative response

   C. Rewarding positive behavior with a positive response

2. How do negative reinforcement and punishment discourage staff motivation? ______________________________

   ____

   ____

3. What is a positive, effective alternative to punishment?

   ____

4. Individual staff members react differently to different types of positive reinforcement. How can correctional supervisors and managers match the right positive reinforcement to the right staff member?

   ____

   ____

5. List three ways to create a friendly work culture.

   ____

   ____

   ____

6. Your chance of __________ your fellow staff increases with the amount of __________ you spend together.

Chapter Six

MAINTAINING OPEN COMMUNICATION

Chapter Objectives

After completing this chapter, you should be able to:

- Explain how to communicate regularly and appropriately with staff.
- Explain how to visit staff in their work areas.
- Explain how to actively listen to staff concerns.
- Describe how to accept constructive feedback from staff.

Today's staff want to know where their organization is headed and they want the chance to share their ideas and opinions. How important is communication in supporting staff motivation? Consider the following case study:

Since his organization's downsizing, Blaine had been busier than ever—too busy to spend time visiting with his staff. When he arrived in the morning, he greeted whomever he happened to see, and he spoke to the rest at the weekly staff meeting. He was just too stressed to deal with anything more.

Blaine didn't realize how his lack of communication affected his staff until his assistant, Max, asked to meet with him. The staff was beginning to wonder what was wrong, Max explained. The only time most of them saw Blaine anymore was at the weekly meeting—where he spent most of his time telling them that they needed to work harder. When staff members tried to bring up issues of their own, Blaine interrupted, squelching their ideas. The staff was afraid that another round of downsizing was in the works.

Blaine had noticed that his department's work was falling off, but he'd attributed it to the increased workload. Now he was beginning to wonder if there could be another reason. . . .

In a different department, Isabella tried to remain positive. Though the recent layoffs had created some extra challenges for her, she always tried to bring out the best in her staff.

"How do you do it?" one of her staff members asked. "Even in our craziest times, you manage to stay positive. We know this is hard, but we always look forward to your comments because they're so helpful. Because of you, we're proud of ourselves!"

Isabella was thrilled to hear that comment. It took extra energy to take care of her staff when she was feeling stressed. But, Isabella knew that if she supported her people, they'd support her.

Maintaining open communication with your staff helps inspire motivation.

Maintaining open communication with your staff helps inspire and maintain their motivation. But open communication means more than just a hurried staff meeting or a quick "good morning" as you walk in the door. Truly open communication involves a number of factors, including:

- Communicating regularly with staff in ways that meet their needs
- Visiting staff in their work areas
- Listening to staff concerns
- Accepting constructive feedback from staff

Communicate Regularly—and Appropriately

"I don't know, I just work here." This may be the punch line to an old joke, but it's also the way many staff feel about their organizations. They simply don't know what's going on. When staff feel uninformed and ignored, they often believe that their contribution to the organization isn't valued. This discourages their motivation. You can support strong motivation by communicating regularly with your staff and by adapting your communication to meet their needs.

Communication in today's workplace should be easy. After all, we have more ways to reach each other than ever before: voice mail and E-mail as well as old standbys like group meetings, memos, and one-on-one conversations. But, unfortunately, *more* communication doesn't necessarily mean *better* communication. Consider the following case study:

Betsy decided that she and her staff should communicate more, so she instituted a weekly meeting. She saw the weekly meeting as her department's primary communication tool—the time when everyone would have the chance to share new information and updates. But after a few months, Betsy learned that her staff didn't like the regular meetings. She couldn't understand their responses—after all, they were communicating! What was the problem? she asked. She was surprised at their responses:

- *Regular hours for her shift in the organization were 7 A.M. to 3 P.M. Betsy had been starting her meeting at 6:30 A.M. on Mondays to get a jump on the day and week. This forced staff to rearrange their kids' day-care and*

and school schedules. She was trying to communicate with her staff on what turned out to be their most stressful morning of the week—and she was causing the stress.

- *By insisting that the weekly meeting be her department's primary means of communication, Betsy stifled some flexibility. When staff had new information, they often held it until the weekly meeting rather than sharing it spontaneously. This meant that some staff were late in receiving information they needed.*
- *The weekly meetings themselves went on for an hour. This was too long for most staff members—they generally stopped paying attention about halfway through.*
- *Staff members also felt that the meetings were too one-sided. Betsy took most of the time delivering her information to her staff. But she left little time for staff members to share information or ask questions. Staff members felt that no one cared about their concerns. They wished that they could hold a second weekly meeting—without Betsy.*

Though Betsy was attempting to communicate regularly with her staff, that communication obviously wasn't succeeding. Betsy's staff needed information more quickly than she was providing it. They also needed to meet with each other when they were less stressed and could concentrate. They needed the opportunity to express their own ideas and opinions.

Managers don't always know staff's communication needs.

As Betsy's example points out, correctional supervisors and managers don't always know staffs' communication needs. How can you find out? The best way is to ask them. Some questions you might consider include:

- Do you feel well-informed about what's

going on in our department? In the organization as a whole?

- Are you receiving information often enough?
- Are you receiving information quickly enough?
- Do you feel that you have a chance to express your thoughts and ideas?
- Do you have any suggestions for how we might improve communication in our department?

Your next step is to determine how you can use all the means of communication available to you to meet these needs. For example, Betsy could have met her staffs' needs by sending out a weekly memo to keep people informed of important new developments. She could have also rescheduled her staff meetings for later in the day, and given staff members more time to speak during the meetings.

Take a Moment . . . 

How do you think your staff would answer the previous questions? List your answers below:

Do you feel well-informed about what's going on in our department? In the organization as a whole? ____________________

____

Are you receiving information often enough? ____________

Are you receiving information quickly enough? ____________

Do you feel that you have a chance to express your thoughts and ideas? ____________________________________

____

Do you have any suggestions for how we might improve communication in our department? ____________________

____

Now have your staff answer the questions and compare your answers. How accurately did you predict their responses?

____

Visit Staff Work Areas

"I just don't know what to do about this parolee," Geraldo confessed to his friend Tania, another parole agent. "He's not letting me know what's happening, and dealing with him is getting more difficult.

"Why don't you tell your supervisor about it?" Tania responded. "Maybe he can help you think of something."

"I don't think he'd understand," Geraldo said sadly. "He spends so much time locked up in his office. I don't think he even understands what we do, and I don't really know him well enough to feel comfortable taking a problem like this to him."

We've seen how important it is for correctional supervisors and managers to get to know their staff in order to be able to offer effective reinforcement. Visiting with staff can inspire motivation as well. But supervisors and managers who remain isolated in their offices will never get to know their staff. To truly understand your staff and what they do—and how well they do it—you need to spend some time with them in their own work areas.

This principle has been called "Manage by Walking Around"—MBWA—though some supervisors' and managers' eyes now glaze over when they hear that term. Though it may sound simple, MBWA involves much more than simple walking. Effective MBWA means taking the time to talk with staff and actively listen to their concerns. To get the most from your MBWA time, follow these guidelines:

Visiting with staff can inspire motivation.

- **Be considerate of your staffs' work schedules**. MBWA shouldn't be intrusive or interruptive. If a staff member seems particularly busy, greet him or her briefly and move on. Save in-depth conversation for another day.

- **Use your MBWA time for constructive enlightenment, not criticism**. It's not a time to reprimand staff for completing tasks incorrectly. Staff will resent your visits if they perceive you as a scolding parent.
- **Allow enough time for MBWA**. Effective MBWA means taking the time to listen to staff and respond with authenticity. If you're in a hurry, these things can't happen.
- **Don't make a big show of MBWA.** You don't have to announce that you're going to start doing it—just gradually weave it into your work style.
- **Don't limit MBWA to your staff**. It's a helpful process for working with your peers and your own supervisor, though your style of MBWA will be different in these situations.
- **Adjust your amount of MBWA to your staffs' preferences**. Suppose you get the impression that your staff find your MBWA burdensome, condescending, or interruptive, and you truly can't find anything you've done wrong. Find another means to communicate with them. Don't completely stop visiting others. Just devote more time and energy to other types of communication.

Of course, the nature of your work environment will affect your MBWA efforts. An active prison yard won't be as conducive to MBWA as a quiet office setting. This doesn't mean that you shouldn't use MBWA. But it does mean that you should adjust the length and timing of your visits and support MBWA with other types of communication.

Take a Moment . . . 

How often do you visit your staff in their work areas during a typical week? ______

____

Do you visit some staff more than others?

____

If you aren't visiting all of them regularly, develop a plan for working regular visits into your work schedule.

Staff Member	Assignment	Time
__________	__________	____
__________	__________	____
__________	__________	____
__________	__________	____
__________	__________	____
__________	__________	____

Listen to Staff Concerns

"I think this old PC has just about had it," Rogers said as she looked at the ancient computer at her organization's front desk. "When it crashes, they'll lose a lot of data."

"Shouldn't you tell your supervisor," Mason asked. "Then she could get us another hard drive, so we could transfer the information before we lose it."

"Why bother?" Rogers said. "She never listens to me anyway."

Don't let communication with your staff become a one-way street.

Don't let communication with your staff become a one-way street. Support their motivation by actively listening to their concerns. Some strategies for improving your listening skills include:

- **Listen actively when staff speak with you in person**. You may tell staff that you have an "open door" policy, but how do you react to them when they walk in that door? Active listening means giving speakers your undivided attention, not finishing up paperwork or planning your next meeting while they talk. Use nonverbal communication to show that you're paying attention. Maintain eye contact with the person speaking, nod to show that you understand what's being said, and ask questions when you don't understand. If possible, come out from behind your desk. Take a seat next to the staff member so that the two of you can sit at the same level. Remember to put the staff member at ease by smiling.
- **Provide communication alternatives**. Some staff members feel perfectly comfortable bringing up their concerns at a weekly staff meeting. Some prefer a private meeting, and others prefer to avoid a meeting altogether and voice their concerns in writing. Provide staff with a variety of means to communicate with you. Some ideas include:
    - *Design a quarterly survey that staff can answer anonymously*. Make sure to include essay-type questions, or a general area

for comments—so that staff don't feel that their responses are limited to multiple-choice questions designed by you.

- *Offer a suggestion box.* Some management consultants recommend eliminating this old standby. But others believe that it remains a useful communication tool if staff know that they can also bring concerns to you in person.

- *Create peer feedback teams.* A staff member might feel more comfortable discussing some issues with a peer rather than a supervisor or manager. Give them the opportunity by setting up peer feedback teams.

  TIP: If you start a peer feedback team, train team members so that they will be prepared to handle various types of complaints. Discuss how issues should be brought to your attention without violating staff confidentiality.

- **Respond to staffs' ideas and opinions.** Staff need to know that their ideas and opinions don't just disappear into a black hole. Try to act on staff suggestions when possible, and when you aren't able to act, let staff know why. Respond to staff by following up with them individually. If the issue is a public one, address them during a meeting or through a memo or newsletter article.

Maintain the trust of your staff.
- **Answer concerns.**
- **Keep confidential requests private.**

- **Show staff that they can trust you.** Trust is vital to open communication. Maintain the trust of your staff by answering their concerns with honest responses and by making sure that confidential communication remains private.

Take a Moment . . .

What alternatives do you currently provide for staff who want to communicate with you? List them below:

____

____

____

____

____

What other means of communicating with you could you offer staff?

____

____

____

____

Accept Constructive Feedback

Don't think of staff comments as complaints; think of them as constructive feedback.

"I don't want any complaining." Our parents might have used this phrase when it was our turn to do the dishes. But it's not a useful attitude for a supervisor or manager to take into the workplace. To remain motivated, your staff need to be able to tell you when things in your department aren't running smoothly and offer their suggestions for improvement. Don't think of these comments as complaints; think of them as constructive feedback.

As a supervisor or manager, you need to be able to accept staff feedback gracefully. To do so, you must be able to distinguish between a staff member with legitimate constructive feedback and someone who's just letting off steam. How can you tell the difference?

What Is Constructive Feedback?

Let your whole staff know that you always welcome open communication—whether it's seen as positive or corrective. True constructive feedback deals with something that can be identified and measured in some way. If Mike says, "Things aren't fair around here," and cannot specifically name some instances, he's probably just letting off steam. Maybe Mike thinks the fact that supervisors get paid more than he does "just isn't fair."

Constructive feedback deals with something that can be identified and measured in some way.

But suppose Sam says, "It's hard to process these offenders without their jackets." He then explains that he can't do his work well or meet his quota because he doesn't receive paperwork from another facility on time. Sam has legitimate constructive feedback.

Some staff members may find it difficult to give you constructive feedback because they believe that it's wrong to "complain." Discuss with them the ways that corrective feedback can help your entire department.

What about the chronic complainers who are just letting off steam? You can help them become constructive critics by following these steps:

- **Help your staff understand the difference between corrective feedback and letting off steam**. Let them know that true feedback will be taken seriously.
- **Stress that pointing out a problem isn't enough**. Staff also need to be part of the

solution. Encourage staff members to suggest a solution when they bring you corrective feedback.

- **Let staff members know that they need to continue to do their best while the situation is being evaluated and possibly improved**. Work shouldn't grind to a halt just because a problem exists.

Take a Moment . . .

When was the last time a staff member in your department gave constructive feedback about some aspect of your department that needed improvement?

How did you respond?

Would you respond differently today?

Think of a problem that you would like to address with your supervisor.

What possible solutions are there for the problem?

Open Communication Shows Respect

Staff believe their work is valued when they understand what's happening in their organization and department and are able to make their ideas and opinions known. So make the effort to develop open communication with your staff. This also shows them that you respect them and their contributions to the organization. Moreover, it helps build their motivation. Strive each day to communicate effectively with your staff and watch your department's performance improve.

Summary

Maintaining open communication with your staff helps inspire and maintain their motivation. Truly open communication involves a number of factors:

- **Communicate regularly with staff in ways that meet their needs**—When staff feel uninformed and ignored, they often believe that their contribution to the organization isn't valued, which discourages their motivation. You can support strong motivation by providing your staff with information about what's going on in the organization and department, and by choosing methods of communicating that are appropriate to their needs.
- **Visit staff in their work areas**—Get to know your staff by visiting them in their work areas, or Manage by Walking Around (MBWA). Use this time as a chance to learn more about your staff, not to correct them, and plan your visits, so they aren't bothersome or disruptive.

- **Listen to staff concerns**—Practice active listening whenever you meet with a staff member. Use nonverbal communication to show that the person speaking has your undivided attention. Provide alternative channels for staff to communicate with you, such as a suggestion box or peer feedback committee, and regularly respond to issues raised.
- **Accept corrective feedback from staff**—When staff bring up issues within your department that need improvement, look on their comments as constructive feedback rather than complaints. Help staff understand the difference between corrective feedback about something identifiable and measurable and just letting off steam. Encourage them to present solutions along with their feedback.

Chapter Six Review

Answers to these questions appear on pages 113–114.

1. What is one of the best ways for correctional supervisors and managers to find out what their staff communication needs are?

 ____

 ____

 ____

2. What does MBWA stand for?

 ____

 ____

3. Effective MBWA involves: taking the time to __________ with staff and to ____________________staff concerns.

4. Two strategies that will help you listen more effectively to staff concerns are:

 ____

 ____

5. Look at staff comments as _________ ____________; don't think of them as complaints.

Chapter Seven

DEALING WITH UNMOTIVATED STAFF

Chapter Objectives

After completing this chapter, you should be able to:

- Identify factors that can lead to poor staff performance.
- Explain what a correctional supervisor or manager can do to help unmotivated staff.
- Describe at least four new techniques to inspire motivation.

Most of us have heard the phrase "an unmotivated staff member" before. But what does it really mean?

> *Cransen looked at her watch and shook her head. Johnson had missed another deadline—the third in as many weeks. Why couldn't he get his work done on time? "I guess he's just not motivated," she thought.*

Motivation comes from inside ourselves.

As we discussed earlier, motivation is an internal state—how can you know what a staff member is or isn't feeling? The fact is, you can't, unless that person tells you.

Why Staff Perform Poorly

Usually, when we believe that a staff member is unmotivated, we base our conclusion on the quality of that person's job performance—poor job performance equals lack of motivation. But are we correct in that assumption? After all, many things besides motivation can affect job performance. Poor job performance may be caused by a number of factors, including:

- Staff members don't understand the expectations for performance.
- They don't have the skills to meet the expectations.
- They don't have the time or resources to do the job properly.
- The expectations for performance are so high that nobody could meet them.

Many things besides motivation can affect job performance.

Learning the Cause of a Performance Problem

How can you discover what the cause of a worker's performance problem is? The best way is to have a talk with your staff member.

Schedule a meeting with the staff member. Describe the ways in which he or she is not meeting performance expectations. Ask the staff member why he or she thinks this is happening, then let him or her respond. You might be surprised by what you learn. Often, staff members realize that a problem exists but don't know what to do about it. They are relieved to have a chance to explain their side of things. The opportunity to work with you to solve the problem will in itself help strengthen the staff member's motivation.

As you speak with the staff member, you may find that she or he might be motivated to achieve in other circumstances. Perhaps the staff member is not currently in the right job. The person may just be more comfortable working independently but must now work with a team. Perhaps you're asking a team-oriented person to work alone.

Maybe the staff member is overqualified and is simply not challenged by the position, or the job is beyond the person's skills and abilities.

At that point, you must make a personnel decision:

- offer training to the staff member to bring him or her up to speed,
- move that person to other job duties, or
- if there is no other alternative, terminate him or her.

Take a Moment . . . 

Think of a staff member who is not meeting expectations for performance. Based on the list given earlier, can you think of an explanation for the person's poor performance? Write it below:

Dealing with Poor Motivation

If you have considered other alternatives and can find no reason for a staff member's poor performance, lack of motivation could be the answer. There are many reasons why a staff member might not be motivated. You can help solve some of these situations but not all of them.

What Can a Correctional Supervisor or Manager Do?

Are you doing everything you can to inspire staff motivation?

First, help the staff member with low motivation. Ask yourself if you are doing everything you can as a supervisor or manager to inspire motivation. Perhaps you haven't conveyed your vision in a way that the staff member understands. Or, maybe you haven't offered a reward that the staff member values. Review the previous chapters of this workbook for more ideas.

Take a Moment . . .

Are you doing all you can to inspire motivation in your less-motivated staff members? Review the following checklist:

Do I . . .

___ Articulate a clear vision for my department or team?

___ Help my staff determine strategic imperatives to meet our department goals?

___ Measure and evaluate my staffs' work in a meaningful way?

___ Recognize staff achievement through a fair reward system?

___ Tell staff what they need to do in order to earn rewards?

___ Offer rewards that my staff members value?

___ Use positive reinforcement instead of negative reinforcement or punishment?

___ Do what I can to create a staff-friendly organizational culture?

Staff motivation can also be affected by personal factors outside the workplace, including:

- Money problems
- Illness or loss of a family member
- Family or marital conflict
- Drug, alcohol, or gambling addiction(s)
- Physical illness
- Chronic depression

Staff motivation can be affected by personal factors.

As a supervisor or manager, it is not your role to counsel staff on personal issues. If you have reason to believe that an outside problem is affecting a staff member, you can suggest that she or he seek professional assistance. Many correctional organizations have assistance programs to which you can refer a staff member for confidential counseling. Check to see what your organization offers.

Remember Your Responsibilities

Even a correctional supervisor or manager who does everything possible to support motivation may still encounter problem staff members. Remember that individuals are ultimately responsible for their own motivation. If a staff member stubbornly decides that he or she hates a job or doesn't care about performance standards, your only choice may be termination.

You may empathize with the troubled staff member. But remember that you have a responsibility to your organization and your team to be sure that all staff maintain high levels of performance. A staff member who is consistently unable to meet performance standards—for whatever reason—will keep your team from meeting its goals and discourage the motivation of other team members. Remember to document all staff performance problems according to your organization's policies and procedures. This way, you will be able to defend a termination should one become necessary.

Will firing a poorly performing staff member destroy the motivation of the rest of your team? Almost never, if you follow proper procedures and keep the situation as professional as possible. Remaining staff are probably aware of the problem and will understand your decision. If the terminated member is difficult to work with, they may even be relieved.

Of course, prevention is better than having to deal with staff in this extreme manner. You can't prevent all personnel problems because people themselves are unpredictable. But making sound hiring decisions and assigning staff to jobs that fit their abilities will greatly increase your chances of motivational success.

Take a Moment . . .

Do you know your organization's procedures for disciplinary action and termination? Outline the procedures that you must follow.

More Ideas for Inspiring Motivation

Try these additional steps to enhance your staffs' abilities to be productive:

- **If possible, eliminate some of the signs of status difference**. Can you make door nameplates the same size? Eliminate reserved parking spaces? Do away with a separate supervisors break room? For some organizations, these and other steps would work and be of help to staff members.

- **Can you also eliminate the signs of distrust around your organization, such as time cards, time clocks, sign-in sheets, etc.?**

If you don't answer the "tough" questions about controversial issues, the gossip mill will.

- **Don't avoid staff's "tough" questions**. If you don't answer questions about possible downsizing, layoffs, and other controversial issues, the gossip mill will. Tough questions don't go away; they only get tougher and meatier until they're dealt with.

- **In establishing rapport with your staff, don't get too close or be too distant**. It's not an easy place to get to, because it's a fine line. But going too far in either direction spells trouble.

- **Develop an attitude that you work as much for your staff as they work for you**. Ask your team members how you can help them do their jobs better. Let them know that you are there to help.

- **Celebrate important anniversaries with your staff**. Recognize a new staff member's first day by introducing the new worker to the staff, having refreshments, taking the new person to lunch. Do whatever you can to make the day special. Also recognize staff members on their birthdays and on their work anniversary dates.

- **Make tasks less boring any time you can. Split up the boring or grunt work**. Don't give it all to the one department member who is new to the organization. What a way to tell someone, "Here's the start of your career."
- **Encourage cross-training whenever you can**. In today's ever-changing workplace, cross-training almost always comes in handy.
- **Take action now**. Don't start practicing the ideas in this workbook next week, "when there'll be less to do." You'll keep putting the whole thing, or at least part of it, off until there is a "better" time. Even if you're having difficulty right now with staff members who are gobbling up your time, begin taking measures to inspire motivation.

Practice the principles in this workbook and augment them with additional knowledge about drawing out the higher and better qualities inherent in all people. You'll be rewarded handsomely with a loyal staff of hard workers who will make you proud and hold you in high esteem.

Take a Moment . . .

Which steps or ideas for motivating your staff can you implement now?

Summary

Many factors can affect staff performance, including:

- Staff don't understand the expectations for performance.
- They don't have the skills to meet the expectations.
- They don't have the time or resources to do the job properly.
- The expectations for performance are so high that nobody could meet them.
- They are capable of meeting expectations but aren't motivated to do so.

The best way to determine the cause of poor performance is to discuss the problem with the staff member. First, eliminate other alternatives for poor performance. If none of these fit, low motivation may be the problem. Ask yourself if you are doing everything you can as a correctional supervisor or manager to inspire and support motivation for this individual. You might try changing the rewards offered or providing more positive reinforcement.

Staff motivation can also be affected by personal factors outside the workplace, including:

- Money problems
- Illness or loss of a family member
- Family or marital conflict
- Drug, alcohol, or gambling addiction(s)
- Physical illness
- Chronic depression

An individual who is consistently unable to meet performance standards—for whatever reason—will keep your team from meeting its goals and discourage the motivation of other team members. Remember to document all staff performance problems according to your organization's procedures so that you will be able to defend a termination if necessary.

Chapter Seven Review

Answers to these questions appear on pages 114–116.

1. Lack of motivation is not the only cause of poor staff performance. List four others.

   ____

   ____

   ____

   ____

2. The best way to learn about the cause of a staff member's personal problem is to talk with:

   A. Your supervisor
   B. One of the counselors
   C. One of your fellow supervisors or managers
   D. The staff member

3. List three personal factors that can affect staff motivation.

   ____

   ____

   ____

4. True/False. Individuals are ultimately responsible for their own motivation.

5. True/False. It is your duty as a correctional supervisor or manager to counsel staff on personal issues when those issues affect workplace performance.

6. True/False. Firing a poorly performing staff member will destroy the motivation of the rest of your team.

7. List four ways to enhance your staff's abilities to be productive.

   ____

   ____

   ____

   ____

Answers to Chapter Reviews

Chapter One Review

1. **False**. Correctional supervisors and managers can only create a work environment that encourages and supports motivation on the part of employees.
2. Today's correctional workers place an **increasing emphasis** on work and working together in teams.
3. **False**. Fear is *not* an effective way to encourage motivation.
4. For many correctional workers, **home life** and the **workplace** are equally hectic.
5. Team situations can discourage staff motivation when the team experiences a number of conflicts or individual members believe that their efforts are ignored or undervalued.

Chapter Two Review

1. The five categories of human needs identified by Abraham Maslow are the following:
   - Self-Actualization
   - Self-Esteem
   - Social/Belonging
   - Safety/Security
   - Physical needs
2. **True**.
3. Working in **teams** can provide us with the opportunity to meet our social needs.

4. According to David McClelland, the three types of needs people hope to satisfy specifically through work include:

   - Love or caring for others as human beings
   - Achievement
   - Power

5. As more people question their desire for **money**, correctional supervisors and managers will need to use other aspects of the work environment to inspire motivation.

Chapter Three Review

1. A vision or mission statement articulates the results you hope your department or team will achieve.

2. **Strategic Imperatives** are limited, specific goals that staff can complete and measure.

3. **Job measures** provide a way to quantify staff progress in meeting strategic imperatives.

4. The guidelines for maintaining staff motivation for a quality program are:

   A. Emphasize that everyone is a **link** in the quality chain.
   B. Allow each staff member to **overrule** everyone when she or he knows that something is not top quality.
   C. Give staff authority, and hold them **accountable** for every decision.
   D. Make results **measurable** and broadcast those results so that everyone

can see progress.

E. Make **quality** part of the process even when it's difficult.

5. Three values that can inspire staff include:

    - Respect for others
    - Honesty and integrity
    - Fairness

Chapter Four Review

1. A **reward** can be effective only if the staff member values what is being offered.

2. A staff member must see a reward as **attainable** for it to be effective.

3. The type of reward that can inspire motivation by showing staff that their hard work is noticed and appreciated is:

    ✓ A. Recognition
    B. Monetary
    C. Attainable
    D. All of the above

4. **False**. You should never praise staff on their personal qualities, only on their *performance*.

5. Four things you can do to keep rewards from backfiring are:

    A. Be as fair as possible in your distribution of rewards.
    B. Monitor staff performance and recognize hard work on the part of all staff members.
    C. Find ways to recognize smaller accomplishments as well as larger ones.

D. Set reasonable performance standards for rewards, and regularly let all staff know how they can reach them.

Chapter Five Review

Page 70 Take a Moment:

__NR__ 1. "Those boxes need to be loaded on the truck in the next hour, or you'll have some explaining to do."

__PR__ 2. "I want to recognize Jacqueline for the wonderful job she did preparing a totally new schedule for the department."

__P__ 3. "Randy, you continue to come to work late—this is the third time in two weeks! I'm putting you on probation."

__NR__ 4. "If you make this many errors on your next report, I'll have to put a note in your personnel file."

1. Match the following terms to the appropriate definition.

   __C__ Positive reinforcement
   __A__ Negative reinforcement
   __B__ Punishment

   A. Rewarding positive behavior by not carrying through on a negative response
   B. Meeting negative behavior with a negative response
   C. Rewarding positive behavior with a positive response

2. Negative reinforcement and punish-

ment can discourage staff motivation by creating a climate of fear, anger, and mistrust.

3. A positive, effective alternative to punishment is **discipline**.

4. Correctional supervisors can match the right positive reinforcement to the right staff member by getting to know staff as individuals.

5. Ways to create a friendly work culture include (choose three):

    - Offering opportunities for education and training
    - Offering flexibility to deal with family issues
    - Respecting the diversity of your staff
    - Accommodating physically challenged staff members (when appropriate)
    - Providing opportunities to socialize outside of work

6. Your chance of **liking** your fellow staff increases with the amount of **time** you spend together.

Chapter Six Review

1. One of the best ways for correctional supervisors and managers to find out about their staffs' communication needs is to ask them. Questions you might ask include:

    - Do you feel well-informed about what's going on in our department? In the organization as a whole?

    - Are you receiving information often

enough?
- Are you receiving information quickly enough?
- Do you feel that you have a chance to express your thoughts and ideas?
- Do you have any suggestions for how we might improve communication in our department?

2. **MBWA** stands for Manage by Walking Around.

3. Effective MBWA involves: taking the time to **talk** with staff and to **actively listen** to staff concerns.

4. Strategies that will help you listen more effectively to staff concerns include (choose two):

   - Listen actively when staff speak with you in person.
   - Provide communication alternatives.
   - Respond to staff ideas and opinions.
   - Show staff that they can trust you.

5. Look at staff comments as **constructive feedback**; don't think of them as complaints.

Chapter Seven Review

1. Lack of motivation is not the only cause of poor staff performance. Other causes include:

   - Staff members don't understand the expectations for performance.
   - They don't have the skills to meet the expectations.
   - They don't have the time or resources to do the job properly.
   - The expectations for performance

are so high that nobody could meet them.

2. The best way to learn about the cause of a staff member's personal problem is to talk with:

   A. Your supervisor
   B. One of your counselors
   C. One of your fellow supervisors or managers
   ✓ D. The staff member

3. Staff motivation can be affected by personal factors outside the workplace, including (choose three):

   - Money problems
   - Illness or loss of a family member
   - Family or marital conflict
   - Drug, alcohol, or gambling addiction(s)
   - Physical illness
   - Chronic depression

4. **True**.

5. **False**. It is *not* your role to counsel staff on personal issues. You can suggest that a staff member seek professional assistance.

6. **False**. If you follow proper policies and procedures and keep the situation as professional as possible, remaining staff should understand your decision.

7. Ways to enhance your staff's abilities to be productive are (choose four):

   - Eliminate some of the signs of status differences in the office.
   - Eliminate the signs of distrust around your organization, such as

time cards, time clocks, sign-in sheets, etc.

- Don't avoid staff's "tough" questions.
- In establishing rapport with your staff, don't get too close or too distant.
- Develop an attitude that you work as much for your staff as they work for you.
- Celebrate important anniversaries with your staff.
- Make tasks less boring any time you can.
- Encourage cross-training whenever you can.
- Take action now.